PRAISE FOR

Thirty-one Secrets of Success

Through this book, Rodney has a way of integrating his intellectual, soulful, and spiritual knowledge by expressing the essentials to 'thriving' vs. the disadvantages to 'just surviving' in life. Through his meticulous and conscientious writing, Rodney utilizes his God-given skills to share the highlights of what God can do when we give Him permission to work in our lives using meditation and belief. I have decided and have given God permission to shower me with abundance because I'm a worthy daughter of the King. Thank you for this clever handbook, Rodney!

~Zinah Scott
Health and Life Coach, Tennessee

Author Rodney Lewis Boyd's latest encouragement book on how to make life better is titled, *Thirty-One Secrets to the not so Secret, Secrets of Success.* This is the third part of his trio of books that began with *How To Live A Maximized Life,* followed by *Biblical Prosperity and Success: Ruminator Style,* and concludes with this latest gem. In the third book, the author continues to encourage the reader to examine themselves in ways that should make us stop and think. The 31 secrets are sometimes ways we randomly overlook in today's busy world, sometimes reminders of what is truly important, and more often nuggets of application for our daily walk in Christ and this world. Each chapter reveals a different 'opportunity' for the reader to glean from Rodney's experience and knowledge and then to apply these secrets to tomorrow and beyond. This is the wonderful conclusion of how to become 'more in Christ,' a better person, and a happier pilgrim as we sojourn our time in this world. I hope a boxed set is offered, as these are wonderful companion pieces to each other.

~Michael Hendrickson
Director/Manager of Wherry Housing

In his book, *Thirty-one Secrets of the not so Secret Secrets of Success*, Rodney Boyd continues his teaching the meaningfulness of God's Word. It is the third book in his trilogy; the first two *How to Live a Maximized Life* and *Biblical Prosperity and Success*. This third book explains each secret in its 31 chapters. Rodney defines and analyzes the prominent words in the stated secret, then encourages the reader to read Old and New Testament verses that support the concept. Rodney breaks down the verses so that the reader can understand and relate the secret to his own life routines. (Each chapter could be a class for study and discussion.) Rodney's Biblical studies and scholarly writings are apparent in his books, and this is no exception. He encourages spiritual thought, understanding, and Bible self-study. While Rodney has organized his *Thirty-one Secrets* book into 31 chapters, he transparently threads his Biblical philosophy through all the "secrets" so that the reader wishes to learn more about how God's messages relate to everyday life. How to accomplish God's purpose is revealed in the *not so Secret, Secrets of Success*.

~Dr. Kay R. Garrard, PhD
Professor Emerita, Middle Tennessee State University

I have been learning from and reading the writings of Rodney Boyd for almost 40 years. He has a way of teaching that explains the Bible and makes scriptures applicable to everyday life. This book does exactly that. It is a roadmap to success with step-by-step procedures infused with Biblical principles and thorough explanations. Rodney shares the plan God has for us to have His provision and success. This is a book that I will keep on my desk as a reference to always be reminded about how to walk in God's provision and have the correct mindset for Biblical success.

~Alison Payne
BS Elementary & Special Ed; M.Ed. School Counseling

THIRTY-ONE SECRETS OF SUCCESS

Also by
Rodney Lewis Boyd

Never Run a Dead Kata
Written that You may Believe
Pro-Verb Ponderings
Speaking and Hearing the Word of God
Chewing the Daily Cud, Vols 1-4
On Earth as it is in Heaven
How to Live a Maximized Life
Biblical Prosperity and Success: Ruminator Style

THIRTY-ONE
SECRETS
TO THE NOT SO SECRET SECRETS
OF SUCCESS

RODNEY LEWIS BOYD

WordCrafts Press

Thirty-one Secrets of Success
Copyright © 2024
Rodney Lewis Boyd

ISBN: 978-1-962218-63-4

Cover concept by David Warren.
Cover design by Mike Parker.

Unless otherwise noted, all scripture quotations are taken from the New American Standard Bible®, Copyright © 1960, 1962, 1963, 1968, 1971, 1972, 1973, 1975, 1977, 1995 by The Lockman Foundation. Used by permission. (www.Lockman.org)

Scripture quotations marked "AMP" taken from the Amplified® Bible, Copyright © 1954, 1958, 1962, 1964, 1965, 1987 by The Lockman Foundation Used by permission. (www.Lockman.org)

Scripture quotations marked "KJV" taken from the King James Version of the Bible, public domain.

All references to "Strong's" refer to Strong's Exhaustive Concordance of the Bible, public domain.

Published by WordCrafts Press
Cody, Wyoming 82414
www.wordcrafts.net

DEDICATION

I dedicate this book to the woman behind my success, my lady, my friend (since 1969) and my wife (since 1972). She is my Pro-Verbs 31 woman who constantly inspires me to be a better man and man of God.

I dedicated this book to my family, Phillip my son, Jamie my daughter-in-law, and Emerson Grace, How Sweet the Sound who keep inspiring me to continue on even though I am an imperfect dad, dad-in-law and Gaggy (G-Ah-Gee).

I dedicate this book to a mentor who changed the trajectory of my life of thinking, Bob Proctor (who has transitioned from life to death back to life again) and many others of like kind.

I dedicated this book to all who have encouraged me over the years as I teach these principles.

And last, **BUT** not least I dedicated this book to my Lord (Kurios, Master, Savior, the one in control of my life) Jesus (God is salvation) Immanuel (God with us) Christ (the Anointed One who is anointed with yoke breaking, burden lifting, oppression removing, healing power of the Holy Ghost) who is the One Who makes me prosperous and successful with an abundant life.

CONTENTS

FOREWORD

Rodney Boyd is one of those charismatic characters that is as memorable as he is persistent. He refuses to quit. He doesn't know how to give up. I'm sure he's tried. I can't eloquently tell you what a source of encouragement he's been to me in my walk with Jesus. As my friend and Sunday School teacher, wise counsel and mentor, man of God and brother in Christ, the position of relationship I think of most when it comes to Rodney (Elder Rod-O) (He was an elder at our church, this was his nickname) is Encourager!

To round out the trilogy of The Success Series, his book, *The Thirty-One Not So Secret, Secrets To Success,* is an extension of his lifestyle of encouragement. Everyone is hoping there's some secret to success, but when we think of secrets, what most of us really want to know... is the shortcut. Rodney explains "Ruminator Style" why the secrets are not short cuts, nor are they really secrets, but rather fundamental truths hidden in plain view by the written Word, authored by God and revealed by the power of the Holy Spirit.

There is no shortcut to reading, comprehending, studying, praying, and obeying. As you read the not so secrets, you'll be challenged and enlightened by Rodney's insights into the Scriptures and God's definition of success. Rodney's done the homework and he's sharing the answers. If you'll be so bold as to apply the not-so-secret, secrets, you'll be blessed by God and the success you experience will be not so secret as well. That could mean success as defined by man or success blessed by strength and power that could only come from Jesus regardless of your circumstances. With Jesus, there's no way you can lose.

~Brad White

INTRODUCTION

The last two books in my Success Trilogy have been thematic about prosperity and success. *How To Live A Maximized Life* speaks of how to live an overcoming, more than conqueror, victorious, abundant, blessed, prosperous and successful lifestyle. Volume Two explored *Biblical Prosperity And Success Ruminator Style*. This book is called *Thirty-One Secrets To The Not So Secret, Secrets Of Success*. The format of the book will be teaching, commentary, and practical application with questions for you to answer. Some chapters will be long, some will be short, and yes, there will be repetition of information. The repetition will reinforce the information about the secrets and act as a safeguard. (Philippians 3:1)

> *The secret things belong to the lord our God, but the things revealed belong to us and to our sons forever, that we may observe all the words of this law.*
>
> ~Deuteronomy 29:29

I try to walk in the things reveled. The secrets are God's wisdom, but this wisdom is "not of this age nor of the rulers of this age" (1 Corinthians 2:6) This wisdom, the secret is a "mystery." (1 Corinthians 2:7) "Things which eye has not seen, and ear has not heard, and which has not entered the heart of man, all that God has prepared for those who love Him." (1 Corinthians 2:9, Isaiah 64:4, Isaiah 65:17) God is the great revealer of mysteries and secrets.

For to us God revealed them through the Spirit (big S, the Holy

Spirit); for the Spirit searches all things, even the depths of God (where the secrets and mysteries are found).
　　　　　　　　　　　　　　　~1 Corinthians 2:10, additions mine

The communication connection between God and humans is the spirit (little s, the human spirit, the lamp of the Lord, Pro-Verbs 20:27) and the Holy Spirit (the Big S that dwells inside of us).

For who among men knows the thoughts of man except the spirit (little s) of the man which is in him? Even so the thoughts of God (including secrets and mysteries) no one knows except the Spirit of God.
　　　　　　　　　　　　　　　~Romans 8:26–27, additions mine

The bottom line is that we can have the *mind of Christ* and are able to receive understanding of the secret and mysteries of God. I believe that God has revealed the *Not So Secret, Secrets Of Success* to us to use in the natural world. Many people (not all people) believe that if you want to be prosperous and successful, all you must do is think about it, have faith for it, speak it aloud, visualize it, and *bam!* it will appear to you. Those people have been labeled those who open their Bible and *"name it and claim it," "blab it and grab it,"* or take your finger, open your Bible, close your eyes, and point to a Scripture, aka *"pop it and pick it."*

Sometimes people will ask me if I am one of those *name it and claim it guys.* I will usually say, *yes... and... no.* The no part is, no I don't believe in manipulating God to give me whatever I want. The yes part is, yes, I do believe that God has given me the power of choice, and I can read His Word, come into agreement with His Word, and *claim (declare)* His Word in my life. I have the power and ability to choose God's will (wishes, desires) in my life, and I also have the power and ability to reject His will (wishes and desires) in my life. I can choose to believe in the Death, Burial, Resurrection (the true Gospel) or to reject it and go to hell. Going to hell is *not* God's will (wish and desire) for me, but by my free will (volition) I can make choices.

WILL: thelēma (thel'-ay-mah)=From the prolonged form of G2309; a determination (properly the thing), that is, (actively) choice (specifically purpose, decree; abstractly volition) or (passively) inclination: - desire, pleasure, will. **G2309: thelō ethelō thel'-o, eth-el'-o**=Either the first or the second form may be used. In certain tenses θελέω theleo thel-eh'-o (and ἐθέλέω etheleō eth-el-eh'-o) are used, which are otherwise obsolete; apparently strengthened from the alternate form of G138; to determine (as an active voice option from subjective impulse; whereas G1014 properly denotes rather a passive voice acquiescence in objective considerations), that is, choose or prefer (literally or figuratively); by implication to wish, that is, be inclined to (sometimes adverbially gladly); impersonally for the future tense, to be about to; by Hebraism to delight in: - desire, be disposed (forward), intend, list, love, mean, please, have rather, (be) will (have, -ling, -ling [ly]).

WILL (BOULOMAI*):* is a strong term that underlines the predetermined (and determined) intention driving the planning (wishing, resolving). In contrast, 2309 (*thélō*) focuses on the *desire* ("wishfulness") behind making an *offer. to "will," that is, (reflexively) be willing: - be disposed, minded, intend, list (be, of own) will (-ing).* (2 Peter 3:9)

Thelema is God's wishes, desires, hinged on our choice. We can choose God's will in many areas of our lives including blessing/life or curse/death. I choose blessing and life, I choose prosperity over poverty, I choose healing over sickness, I choose peace over anxiety. I choose to believe God's Word over men's traditions that nullify the Word of God making it ineffectual. Yes, I choose Biblical Prosperity and Success over the world's/the d-evil's poverty and failure.

Thy Kingdom (rule, realm, reign, foundation of power come (to earth) Thy will (wish, desire) be done (manifested) on earth (where there is sin, sickness, dis-ease, dis-comfort, dis-stress, dys-function, the curse, poverty and any other negative thing) AS IT IS (the blueprint, the template, the mirror image) in heaven (where there is forgiveness, healing, ease, comfort, no stress, function, blessing, prosperity and anything else that is positive.

~Matthew 6:10 with emphasis,
additions, commentary mine, Ruminator Style

Those who are in opposition to this type of mentality mistakenly call it the *prosperity gospel.* Of course, at one time, the Apostle Paul wrote to a group of believers who were believing what he called *"a different gospel"* but then added quickly that there is *really not a "different gospel."* (Galatians 1:6–9 with emphasis, additions, commentary mine, Ruminator Style)

Now I (Paul) make known to your, brethren (true believers), the gospel (Good News) which I preached to you (so faith could come), which you also received (so they could become children of God) , in which also you stand, by which you are saved, if you hold fast the word which I preached to you, unless your believed in vain. For I delivered to you as of first importance what I also received, that Christ (Jesus, the Anointed One) died (D) for our sins according to the Scriptures (the Word of God), and that He (Jesus the Anointed One) was buried (B), and that He was raised (R) from the dead according to the Scriptures (the Word of God).

~1 Corinthians 15:1-4, additions mine

The Gospel, in a nutshell, is found in 1 Corinthians 15:1–5.

I like to call the Gospel (the Good News), the D.B.R., the Death, Burial, Resurrection, nothing more, nothing less. It is not D.B.R. plus good works. It is not D.B.R. plus some cosmic energy of the universe. It is not D.B.R plus some elaborated system that attracts prosperity and success to you. No, it is D.B.R. plus grace, faith, the gift of God and not "on the basis of deeds/works" that we have done in righteousness (our own self-righteousness)! (Ephesians 2:8–10, Titus 3:5)

These principles that I am about to outline for you to study daily for thirty-one days will work even if you are not a believer. I believe that they will work for an atheist, for an agnostic, for other religions. I believe that they will work for denominations, sects, cults, heresies, world religions, etc. I *don't* believe that *the full potential, peace, and joy* will be realized, but the secrets that are not so secret are not based on your goodness, your righteousness, your deserving success, but when combined with the anointing of the Holy Spirit, God's Word, and God's will (His wish and desire) on earth as it is in heaven the potential is optimized.

The format for the book is thirty-one principles of success laid out for thirty-one days. I believe that at the end of the thirty-one days you will have in your arsenal what you need to be prosperous and successful. Some chapters you can just read, some will be designed for you to look up Scriptures, fill in the blanks, and study.

NOTE: While the title speaks of thirty-one days, you may spend a week on one principle, and it could turn into thirty-one secrets in three hundred sixty-five days.

PROSPERITY: Having enough to meet your needs (not your greed) and an overflow to help others.

SUCCESS: Accomplishing the purposes of God in your life and helping others to accomplish their purposes.

There are many books, movies, teachers talking about *the secret* to success. They speak a lot about *the universe* giving you what you want. I am talking about having a relationship with *the Creator of the universe* Who loves me and has a plan and purpose for my life, which is far better than trusting in a distant impersonal universe.

~Rodney Lewis Boyd, 2024

DELIGHT YOURSELF IN THE LORD

Delight yourself in the Lord and He will give you the desires of your heart.

~Psalm 37:4

DELIGHT: **'ânag (aw-nag')**=A primitive root; to be soft or pliable, that is, (figuratively) effeminate or luxurious: - delicate (-ness), (have) delight (self), sport self.

To get ready for the desires of your heart you must first be willing to be shaped by the Lord for His purposes.
1. Be soft to the Lord
2. Be pliable to the Lord
3. Be effeminate or luxurious to the Lord
4. Be delicate to the Lord
5. Sport yourself to the Lord

NOTE: To "be effeminate or luxurious" does not mean for a man to be sexually sensual to the Lord, but to yield your will to the Lord.

This first secret of success is not based on selfishness. The focus is not on *what the Lord can do for you* but *what you can do for the Lord.*

LORD (Hebrew): yehôvâh (*yeh-ho-vaw'*)=from H1961; (the) *self-Existent* or eternal; *Jehovah,* Jewish national name of God: - Jehovah, the Lord. **H1961: hâyâh (*haw-yaw'*)**=A primitive root (compare H1933); to *exist*, that is, *be* or *become, come to pass* (always emphatic, and not a mere copula or auxiliary): - beacon, X altogether, be (-come, accomplished, committed, like), break, cause, come (to pass), continue, do, faint, fall, + follow, happen, X have, last, pertain, quit (one-) self, require, X use.

LORD (Greek): Kurios (*koo'-ree-os)*=From κῦρος kuros (*supremacy*); *supreme* in authority, that is, (as noun) *controller;* by implication *Mr.* (as a respectful title): - God, Lord, master, Sir

God is like the C.E.O. (Chief Executive Officer), the head of the Universal Creation, the Controller, the one in control, the head, where the buck stops. When God speaks we say, "Yes, Sir!" This is the one who we "delight ourselves in."

The word delight simply means to makes yourself pliable to Him in all your dreams, visions, goals, imaginations, inspirations, thoughts, ideas, goals, and plans. I believe that the phrase "delight yourself in the Lord" means that you are positioning yourself to receive the things that God has placed in your heart. I believe that to "delight yourself in the Lord" is preparing yourself to be aware of the things that will be attracted in your life to be prosperous (enough to meet your needs and an overflow to help others) and successful (accomplishing the purposes of God in your life).

GIVE: nâthan (naw-than')=A primitive root; to give, used with great latitude of application (put, make, etc.): - add, apply, appoint, ascribe, assign, X avenge, X be ([healed]), bestow, bring(-forth, hither), cast, cause, charge, come, commit consider, count, + cry, deliver (up), direct, distribute do, X doubtless, X without fail, fasten, frame, X get, give (forth, over, up), grant, hang(up), X have, X indeed, lay (unto charge, up), (give) leave, lend, let (out), + lie, lift up, make, + O that, occupy, offer, ordain, pay, perform, place, pour, print, X pull, put (forth), recompense, render, requite, restore, send (out), set (forth), shew, shoot forth (up). + sing, + slander, strike,[sub-] mit, suffer, X surely, X take, thrust, trade, turn, utter, + weep, X willingly, + withdraw, +would (to) God, yield.

NOTE: There is cause and effect to the Lord giving you the desires with the "cause" being delighting yourself to the Lord and the effect being the Lord giving you "the desires of your heart" I believe that this giving is two-fold.

> *"Delight yourself in the Lord and He will give you the desires of your heart."*
>
> ~Psalm 37:4

Realize that He (the Lord) will (1) plant in you desires (2) bring to pass your dreams, visions, goals, imaginations = desires of your heart. Always remember that success is **NOT** winning the Rat Race, that only makes you the *#1 Rat*, but *success* is accomplishing the purposes of God in your life as you yield your will to Him like a potter molding the clay for His purposes. (Jeremiah 18:6)

> *"Can I not, O house of Israel, deal with you as this potter does? Declares the Lord. Behold, like the clay in the potter's hand, so are you in My hand, O house of Israel."*
>
> ~Jeremiah 18:6

In Psalm 37:1, the rats are called evildoers (doers of evil) and wrongdoers (doers of wrong). We are told to "fret not" and "do not be envious" because of the rats. People who fail constantly look at others and their seemingly success.

DESIRES: mish'âlâh (*mish-aw-law'***)**=From H7592; a *request:* - desire, petition. **H792: shâ'al shâ'êl (***shaw-al', shaw-ale'__***=A** primitive root; to *inquire*; by implication to *request*; by extension to *demand:* - ask (counsel, on), beg, borrow, lay to charge, consult, demand, desire, X earnestly, enquire, + greet, obtain leave, lend, pray, request, require, + salute, X straitly, X surely, wish.

Desires are the expression of what we want. I often ask people, "What Do you really want?" What I am really saying is, "What do you really desire?" When someone struggles with coming up with that answer, most likely, they have not delighted themselves, "in the Lord."

They are being torn between the flesh and the spirit. When I have a client that wants more in their lives, I have a series of questions:
Are you merely satisfied with your life? (Philippians 4:12-13)

NOTE: Satisfaction, many times, is just settling for whatever happens in your life. Don't confuse *contentment* with *satisfaction*.

- Are you merely surviving or are you thriving?
- **NOTE**: Surviving is just getting by in life. Thriving is living exceedingly, abundantly above all that you can think or ask. (Ephesians 3:20)
- What do you really want? (Philippians 4:11, Psalm 23:1)

NOTE: Wanting is not a bad thing. If you are wanting (because of lack) then you may need to check out your relationship with your shepherd. In Him you do not lack anything.

- What are you willing to do to get what you really want? (James 2:16, James 1:22)

NOTE: You can believe and have faith all day long, but if you don't put your faith into action, then all you have is a desire that will not be fulfilled.

- What are you reasons for not getting what you really want? (Hebrews 5:14, Pro-Verbs 16:14, Isaiah 1:18)

NOTE: We have our senses trained/exercised to discern both good and evil. Everything has a purpose and by reason we can determine that purpose. The problem is when we use reason and logic as an excuse for not accomplishing those purposes. God is not against reason.

- What are your excuses for not getting what you really want? (Romans 1:20–21, Romans 2:1–29, Luke 14:18, Genesis 3:8–13)

NOTE: Excuses are reasons gone bad. What may appear to be reasonable in our minds, turns quickly into an excuse to escape the consequences for our choices.

- Who do you blame for not getting what you really want? (Genesis 3:8-13, John 11:21, Job 2:9, Ephesians 4:31–32)

NOTE: The blame game is as old as the Garden experience. Blame is the mother of all excuses.

- What are the mountains, obstacles and obstructions standing in your way of getting what you really want? (Mark 11:22–26)

NOTE: If you are going to have "faith in God constantly" (Mark 11:22 Amplified Bible) then you are going to have to deal with the mountains of impossibilities in your life, by not doubting, believing, speaking directly to them and telling them what to do and where to go *as* you forgive (let it go, let it drop, loose it, leave it) Triple AAA Style, A=Anything A=Against A=Anyone. If you don't you will always have mountains, obstacles, and obstructions standing in the way of you getting what you really want.

> *"My God (the Lord) shall give you (plant in you and bring to pass) the desires (what you really want) of your heart (the mind, the core of who you are)."*
>
> ~Psalm 37:4, addition mine

Starting off these *"not so secrets of the secret of success"* we will consistently come across various Scriptures that links the secrets together and keeps us focused on the prize that we desire.

Remember that a *desire is not a lust*, but *what you want* because *that is what God wants for you.*

What you think, what you speak, and what you do will manifest what you really want. Once you figure out what you really want and then submit it to the Lord, you will figure out what you are willing to do to get what you really want.

"As a man thinketh in his heart/mind **SO** *he* **IS**.*"*
~Pro-Verbs=Positive-Actions 27:3 with emphasis,
additions, commentary mine, Ruminator Style

"...out of the abundance (overflow) of the heart/mind the mouth **SPEAKS**.*"*
~Luke 6:45 with emphasis,
additions, commentary by me, Ruminator Style)

"Faith (what/Who we believe, trust in, cling to, rely on, adhere to, cleave to) without corresponding actions (on our part) is of none effect (dead/lifeless)."
~James 2:17 Weymouth Translation with emphasis,
additions, commentary by me, Ruminator Style

OF YOUR HEART: lêb *(labe)*=A form of H3824; the *heart;* also used (figuratively) very widely for the feelings, the will and even the intellect; likewise for the *centre* of anything: - + care for, comfortably, consent, X considered, courag [-eous], friend [-ly], ([broken-], [hard-], [merry-], [stiff-], [stout-], double) heart ([-ed]), X heed, X I, kindly, midst, mind (-ed), X regard ([-ed)], X themselves, X unawares, understanding, X well, willingly, wisdom. **H3824: lâbab** *(law-bab')*=A primitive root; properly to *be enclosed* (as if with *fat*); by implication (as denominative from H3824) to *unheart*, that is, (in a good sense) *transport* (with love), or (in a bad sense) *stultify;* also (as denominative from H3834) to *make cakes:* - make cakes, ravish, be wise.

The heart is the core of who we are. In the *physical*, the heart is the pump that circulates blood through the body for life.

HEART: A hollow muscular organ that pumps the blood through the circulatory system by rhythmic contraction and dilation, In vertebrates there may be up to four chambers (as in humans), with two atria and two ventricles

In our *spiritual* life, the heart is the core and center of our being.

It can be called our human spirit, the innermost man, the lamp of the Lord. When Adam and Eve sinned, committed high, treason via disobedience in the Garden (Genesis 3:1–24) the heart was corrupted, and humans needed heart surgery with a heart replacement. The heart went from a heart of flesh to a heart of stone and needed to get back to a heart of flesh once again. When people speak of the heart, they say things like:

1. The heart just wants what the heart wants.
2. I'm just following my heart.

The problem with the heart wanting what it wants and you following your heart is the condition of the heart. We need a heart transplant.

"The heart is more deceitful than all else and is desperately sick; who can understand it."

~Jeremiah 17:9

1. Deceitful about all things
2. Desperately wicked
3. Who can know it (the heart)?

"Moreover, I will give you a new heart and put a new spirit within you; and I will remove the heart of stone from your flesh and give you a heart of flesh. I will put My spirit within you and cause you to walk in My statues , and you will be careful to observe My ordinances."
~Ezekiel 36:26–27

God will not force on you a new heart. Like anything in the Kingdom of God, he will not overthrow your will. In John 3:16, God so loved you that He gave Jesus to die in your place. This sacrifice is for whosoever *believes* in Jesus, and you must *choose to believe*; however, He will not *force* you to *believe*. The same goes for a heart transplant.

God's examination of the heart and spirit is this:

"I the Lord, search the heart, I test the mind, even to give to each man according to his ways, according to the results of his deeds."
~Jeremiah 17:10

This is us signing the paperwork and giving God permission for heart surgery.

> *"Search me, O God, and know my heart; Try me and know my anxious thoughts ; and see if there be any hurtful way in me and lead me in the everlasting way."*
> ~Psalm 139: 23–24

The not so secret, secret of success is to delight yourself in the Lord and then act based on the desires that He has placed in your heart of flesh.

LEARN THE ART OF MEDITATION

This book of the law shall not depart from your mouth, but you shall meditate on it day and night, so that you may be careful to do according to all that is written in it; for then you will make your way prosperous, and then you will have success.

~Joshua 1:8

There is a direct link to prosperity and success to the Word of God and your mouth and your actions.

Meditation is not just emptying your mind of everything and thinking of nothing while you chant a mantra or drone on with a specific sound, "ooooommmmmmmm." It is designed to remove the distractions from your mind and then dwell on solutions.

THIS BOOK OF THE LAW: This is in reference to the first five books of the Old Testament called the Pentateuch including, Genesis, Exodus, Leviticus, Number and Deuteronomy (aka as the Jewish Torah) There are around 613 principles/laws/codes about how to live a prosperous and successful life.

SHALL NOT DEPART FROM YOUR MOUTH: This does not mean that you can't speak forth the Word/Law out of your mouth, but to keep the Words close to you as you "meditate" on them by muttering under your breath. When people are at the Wailing Wall in Jerusalem, you will notice that some rock back and forth as they mutter their prayers, this is called "shuckling." Keeping the Word close to you in your mind (meditation), praying and speaking with your mouth keeps

God's commands/law/principles/codes centered and focused.

Phylacteries are small leather box containing Hebrew texts written on vellum (prepared animal skin or membrane, typically used as writing paper) and worn on the wrist/and or the forehead, during prayer as a reminder of the commands/law/principles and codes.

BUT: In contrast to not keeping the Law in your mouth.

YOU SHALL MEDITATE: The word *shall*, indicates that this meditation is not an option, you shall do it if you want the desired results.

MEDITATE: hâgâh (*haw-gaw'*)= A primitive root to *murmur* (in pleasure or anger); by implication to *ponder:* - imagine, meditate, mourn, mutter, roar, X sore, speak, study, talk, utter.

The idea is to think about the commands/law/principles and codes and to mutter/utter them under your breath as you "ruminate" on the Word like a cow or any other animal that is a ruminate does with the "cud." A ruminant is any animal that chews food, swallows it as it goes through four stomachs (chambers) and then regurgitates it back up in the form of a cud. The ruminant then chews the cud over and over again like a piece of chewing gum with a contemplative look about them.

As stated before, Biblical meditation is not just emptying your mind of everything and thinking about nothing like other forms of meditation. No, your empty your mind on purpose of all that is swirling around in your head and distracting you and focus on God and His Word and His purposes in your life. You begin to think God thoughts, speak God thoughts and act upon those thoughts. Every thought that is contrary to God thoughts you take captive and cast down those imaginations. (2 Corinthians 10:3–7)

ON IT: The commands/law/principles and codes.

DAY AND NIGHT: This means all the time and not just on the

Sabbath or Sunday mornings. I believe that this means 7/24/365, all the time. I don't believe that it means that you are meditating 24 hours a day, but like the Word says, "pray without ceasing" (I Thessalonians 5:17), it means at *all times be on the ready with the Word.*

SO THAT YOU MAY BE CAREFUL TO DO: Sometimes we get careless with the Word of God in our lives and forget that,

> *Faith without corresponding actions (works/deeds) is of none effect (dead).*
> ~James 2:17 Weymouth Translation with emphasis, additions and commentary mine, Ruminator Style

ACCORDING TO ALL THAT IS WRITTEN IN IT: Your meditation is based on commands/law/principles and codes found in the Bible/The Word of God.

FOR THEN: After meditation you are ready to put into actions what you are "careful to do".

YOU: Many times, we expect God to do everything for us, but here we see that we have the responsibility to put into action the Word in our lives. In place of the word "you" write your name and say it aloud when quoting this verse. For example, "This book of the law shall not depart from my mouth, but I will meditate on it day and night so that I, Rodney Lewis Boyd will be careful to do according to all that is written in it, for then Rodney Lewis Boyd…"

WILL MAKE YOUR WAY PROSPEROUS: Again, note that it is you, not God, making your way prosperous. I believe that God will give you (plant in you and bring to pass) desires, goals, dreams, visions, imaginations, inspirations, thoughts, ideas, goals and plans of things to do and the cause and effect as you put your faith in to action *you* will make *your* way prosperous.

Remember our definition of prosperity, is we will have enough to meet our needs (not our greed) and an overflow (aka abundance) to help others.

AND THEN: The cause and effect of making your way prosperous.

YOU WILL HAVE SUCCESS: Success is defined as accomplishing the purposes of God in our lives. One verse even says that they will have *"good success."*

The context for this prosperity and good success is crossing over to "possess the promised land." Eight times they were told to be "strong and courageous" and one time it says to be *"strong and very courageous."* (Deuteronomy 31:6–7, Deuteronomy 31:23, Joshua 1:6,7,9,18 and Joshua 10:25.

The reason that they were being prepared to be "strong and courageous" is because they would have every opportunity to be weak and discouraged. They would facing giants in the land and even though the land was promised to them, they still had to take it, and there would be a possibility that they would be in poverty and failure if they were not strong and courageous.

So it is with every endeavor that you attempt from business, school, marriage, sports, (fill in the blank).

BE A GO-GIVER AND NOT A GO-GETTER

Give, and it will be given to you: good measure, pressed down, shaken together, and running over, shall men give into your bosom. For with the same measure that you sue, it will be measured back to you.

~Luke 6:38

Bob Proctor, who was a pioneer in the self-help industry (recently passed away at 85 years old) was working with another pioneer who was one of his mentors, Earl Nightingale, and gleaned from Earl many wonderful ideas. At one point Bob was ready to leave the nest and start his own company. At the Nightingale-Conant company, they charged for every piece of paper that went out of the building, but Bob wanted to do it differently, by giving away materials for free. In this day and age, I do the same thing via email, but at that time, there were no emails. I understand charging for paper/books. Someone once said that the Gospel was given to us for free, so we need to do as Jesus said, *"freely you received, freely give."* (Matthew 10:18) Of course, those who like to quote this verse are looking for you give them something for free, but I like to remind them that, "the Gospel is free, but printing costs." As Bob was about to embark on his own personal journey, a person said to him, "Oh, so you are one of those go-getters." Bob responded back, "No, I am a go-giver."

GIVE: didōmi (*did'-o-mee*)=A prolonged form of a primary verb (which is used as an alternate in most of the tenses); to *give* (used in a very wide application, properly or by implication, literally or figuratively; greatly modified by the connection): - adventure, bestow, bring forth, commit, deliver (up), give, grant, hinder, make, minister, number, offer, have power, put, receive, set, shew, smite (+ with the hand), strike (+ with the palm of the hand), suffer, take, utter, yield.

Give and it shall be given to you, good measure pressed down, shaken together and running over shall men give into your boson. For by your standard of measure it will be measured to you in return.
~Luke 6:38

Give, and [gifts] will be given to you; good measure, pressed down, shaken together, and running over will they pour into [the pouch formed by] the boson [of your robe and sued as a bag]. For with the measure, you deal out [with the measure you use when you confer benefits on others], it will be measured back to you.
~Luke 6:38 Amplified Bible

Some call this the law of reciprocity, sowing and reaping, seed time and harvest, seed faith, casting bread on the water and coming back on every wave. The idea is that there is a cycle in giving and that cycle is not limited to money, but in everything that you have and give out, you can expect a return on your investment.

Can you imagine a farmer withholding seed from the soil and expecting a harvest? Can you imagine a farmer with a silo full of seed and a farm of fertile soil waiting for the seed while the seed rots in the silo? Can you imagine soil that is rocky and weed infested producing anything? That is why God initiated the natural laws of the universe. So many people are Go-Getters, and they wonder why their business fails, why their relationships fail, why their sales have dried up, why their dreams, visions, imaginations, inspirations, thoughts, ideas, goals, and plans are depleted. The root of failures goes back to whether they are *Go-Givers* or *Go-Getters*.

SEED: A flowering plant's unity of reproduction (of like kind), capable (with potential) of developing into another such plant.

"While the earth remains, seedtime and harvest, and cold and heat, and summer and winter, and day and night shall not cease."
~Genesis 8:22

If you are reading this right now, then the earth still remains, and the principle/secret of being a *Go-Giver* still remains.
God was a *Go-Giver* and not a *Go-Getter*.

For God so loved the world that He **GAVE** *His only begotten Son (Seed) that whosoever should believe (trust in, cling to, rely on, adhere to, cleave to) in Him (Jesus) should not perish (have no harvest) but have everlasting (eternal, a long, long, time) life (harvest that comes with the seed planted).*
~John 3:16, emphasis, additions, and commentary mine, Ruminator Style)

When Jesus gave his final orders to His followers, He commissioned them to *GO*. Theologians call this the "Great Commission." I like to call it *The Great GO-mission*.

GO *therefore and make disciples of all the nations, baptizing them in the name of the Father and the Son and the Holy Spirit, teaching them to observe all that I commanded you; and lo, I am with your always, even to the end of the age.*
~Matthew 28:19–20, emphasis mine

Can you imagine if the followers of Jesus kept to themselves his teaching for themselves? There would be no Christianity, there would be no churches, there would be nothing. If the first century followers of Jesus were nothing but *Go-Getters*, then being a Christ Follower would have not gone beyond the first century. We will learn more secrets when we talk about the laws of sowing and reaping.

LEARN TO WALK IN THE FAVOR OF GOD

My son, do not forget my teaching, but let your heart keep my commandments, for length of days and years of life and peace they will add to you. Do not let kindness and truth leave you, bind them around your neck. Write them on the tablet of your heart so you will find favor and good report/repute in the sight of God and man."
~Pro-Verbs 3:1–4, addition mine

The book of Proverbs is a book of advice from a father to a son on how to live out his life. It is one of the first success books, the first self-help books written. I like to call it the book of **PRO-VERBS,** the book of **PRO=POSITIVE VERBS=ACTIONS**, the book of positive action.

FAVOR: chên (*khane*)=From H2603; *graciousness,* that is, subjectively (*kindness, favor*) or objectively (*beauty*): - favour, grace (-ious), pleasant, precious, [well-] favoured. **H2603: chânan (*khaw-nan'*)**=A primitive root (compare H2583); properly to *bend* or stoop in kindness to an inferior; to *favor, bestow*; causatively to *implore* (that is, move to favor by petition): - beseech, X fair, (be, find, shew) favour (-able), be (deal, give, grant (gracious (-ly), intreat, (be) merciful, have (shew) mercy (on, upon), have pity upon, pray, make supplication, X very.

GOOD REPORT/REPUTE/UNDERSTANDING: śekel śêkel (*seh'-kel, say'-kel*)=From H7919; *intelligence*; by implication *success:* - discretion, knowledge, policy, prudence, sense, understanding, wisdom, wise. **H7919: śâkal (*saw-kal'*)**=A primitive root; to *be* (causeatively *make* or *act*) *circumspect* and hence *intelligent:* – consider, expert, instruct, prosper, (deal) prudent (-ly), (give) skill (-ful), have good success, teach, (have, make to) understand (-ing), wisdom, (be, behave self, consider, make) wise (-ly), guide wittingly.

Back in 1993, I graduated from a master's program in Speech-Pathology. My plan/goal was to be a Medical Speech Pathologist, even though I also had a teaching certification for kindergarten through twelfth grade. A godly lady spoke into my life, from the book of Pro-Verbs and she quoted Pro-Verbs 3:1–4 and then focused on verse four. "So you will *find favor and good report/repute/understanding in the sight of (1) God (2) man.*"

She then spoke, I believe prophetically, to me that with this favor with God, that I would have favor with the doctors, nurses, hospital personnel that I came into contact in my job. For thirty-one years I saw that word to be manifested in my life. That word continues to this day even after I retired from Speech Pathology, into every area of my life.

As with all of the principles of success, they are hinged on the principle of cause and effect. You *exercise* the cause and God will *exhibit* the effect. We will look at sowing and reaping in another lesson.

"*…whatever (good, bad, ugly) a man sows this he will also reap.*"
~Galatians 6:7, addition mine

PRO-VERBS 3:1–10

1. Don't forget the father's teaching
2. Let/Allow your heart to keep the father's commandments
   a. What should the son not forget? (Pro-Verbs 3:1)
   b. What should the son allow his heart to keep? (Pro-verbs 3:1)
   c. What two things will be added? (Pro-Verbs 3:1)
   d. What will be added to you? (Pro-verbs 3:2)

NOTE: The cause and effect is that you will have length of days and years of life

3. Don't let kindness and truth to leave you

4. Bind kindness and truth around your neck (so they will always be with you wherever you go and whatever you do in life, including business)

5. Write them on the tablet of your heart (the core of who you are)

    a. What should you not let kindness and truth do? (Pro-Verbs 3:3)

    b. Where should you bind kindness and truth? (Pro-Verbs 3:3)

    c. Where should you write kindness and truth? (Pro-Verb 3:3)

    d. When you remember the teachings and allow your heart to keep the commandments, and not let kindness and truth leave you, and you find truth and kindness around your neck, and write kindness and truth on the tablet of your heart, what will you find? (Pro-Verbs 3:4)

    e. Where will this favor that you find be manifested? (Pro-Verbs 3:4)

NOTE: The cause and effect are that you will find favor and good report/repute/understanding in the sight of God and man.

6. Trust in the Lord with all your heart

7. Do not lean on your own understanding

8. In all your ways acknowledge Him

    a. What should you do with all of your heart? (Pro-Verbs 3:5)

    b. How much of your heart should you use to trust in the Lord? (Pro-Verbs 3:5)

    c. What should you not lean on? (Pro-Verbs 3:5)

    d. In what should acknowledge? (Pro-verbs 3:6)

    e. When you trust in the Lord with all of your heart, and do not lean on your own understanding and acknowledge Him in all your ways, what will He do (the cause and effect)? (Pro-verbs 3:6

NOTE: The cause and effect are that he will make your paths straight.

9. Do not be wise in your own eyes

10. Fear the Lord

11. Turn away from evil
    a. Where should you not be wise? (Pro-Verbs 3:7)
    b. Who should you fear? (Pro-Verbs 3:7)
    c. What should you do when you fear the Lord? (Pro-Verbs 3:7)
    d. When you are not wise in your own eyes, and you fear the Lord and turn away from evil, what will it be? (Pro-Verbs 3:8)

NOTE: The cause and effect are that it will (1) be healing to your body (2) refreshment to your bones

12. Honor the Lord from your wealth and the first of all your produce (tithing and giving)
    a. What should you honor the Lord with? (Pro-Verbs 3:9)
    b. What will be the cause and effect of honoring the Lord from your wealth? (Pro-Verbs 3:10)

NOTE: Your vats will overflow with new wine. Overflow is abundance and that is manifestation of prosperity and success. Produce and fruit/grapes (your lively hood, your income, your wealth, your money) will be into the barns and vats (banks/savings). Notice that there will be plenty and overflow (abundance)

NOTE TO THE NOTE: Walking in this thing called favor has a direct impact on your spiritual relationship, emotional well-being, and your physical health.

WALK IN FULL DISCLOSURE

*He who has My commandments and keeps them is the one who loves Me; and he who loves Me will be loved by My Father and I will love him and will **disclose** Myself to him."*
~John 14:21, emphasis mine

The person who has My commandments and keeps the is the one who [really] loves Me; and whoever [really] loves Me; will be loved by My Father, and I [too] will love him and will show (reveal, manifest) Myself to him. [I will let Myself be clearly seen by him and make Myself real to him.]
~John 14:21 Amplified Bible

a. What must you do when you have the commandments? (John 14:21)

b. Who does the one who has and keep the commandments love? (John 14:21)

c. Who will you be loved by when you love Jesus? (John 14:21)

d. Who else will you be loved by when the Father loves you? (John 14:21)

e. Who will be disclosed to you when you keep the commandments, loves Jesus and the Father? (John 14:21)

When you are trying to be successful (accomplishing the purposes of God in your everyday life), it is a good thing to be on the same page as the C.E.O. (aka God). You want full disclosure, revelation, and manifestation that only comes by a connection with the one in charge. For our purposes that is God, but in business, which could be managers, bosses, C.E.O., your pastor, husbands/wives/children, etc.

Many people know the commandments, the plan, the protocol, but few people keep to the plan. One of the secrets to success is not only keeping to the plan but love for the Master Planner.

1. He (you) who has My (Jesus) commandments
2. And keeps them (not only has them, knows them, memorized them)
3. He (you) it is who loves Me (Jesus)
4. And he (you) who loves Me (Jesus)
5. Will be (cause and effect) be loved by My (Jesus) Father (who art in heaven)
6. And I (Jesus) will love him (you)
7. And will (cause and effect) disclose, manifest, reveal Myself (Jesus) to him (you).

They key to disclosure, revelation and manifestation is **KEEPING THE COMMANDMENTS.**

KEEPING: tēreō (*tay-reh'-o)*=From τηρός teros (a *watch*; to *guard* (from *loss* or *injury*, properly by keeping *the eye* upon; and thus differing from G5442, which is properly to *prevent* escaping; and from G2892, which implies a *fortress* or full military lines of apparatus), that is, to *note* (a prophecy; figuratively to *fulfil* a command); by implication to *detain* (in custody; figuratively to *maintain*); by extension to *withhold* (for personal ends; figuratively to *keep unmarried*): - hold fast, keep (-er), (ob-, pre-, re) serve, watch.

For example, your boss tells you to see five clients before lunch, and you don't start seeing clients until after lunch. You are not keeping the commandments and you get no sales which means you will not be prosperous, and you will not be successful.

COMMANDMENTS: entolē (*en-tol-ay')*=From G1781; *injunction*, that is, an authoritative *prescription:* - commandment, precept. **G1781: entellomai (*en-tel'-lom-ahee)*=** to *enjoin:* - (give) charge, (give) command(-ments), injoin.

NOTE: The Law, the Word, the Code, the Commandments, and the *meditation* (ruminating) and *keeping* of them are linked to *prosperity and success* (Joshua 1:8)

> *This book of the Law (The Word of God) shall not depart from Rodney Lewis Boyd's mouth (keep speaking the Word)* **BUT** *(in contrast to) Rodney Lewis Boyd shall meditate (ponder, think about, ruminate, mutter under your breath) on it (The Law/Word of God) day and night (7/24/365)* **SO** *(the reason for meditating on the Word) that Rodney Lewis Boyd may be careful (if you are NOT careful, you will not meditate on the Word) to do (action on what you have been meditating on)* **FOR THEN** *(at that moment) Rodney Lewis Boyd will make (action) his way prosperous (wealthy, affluent, rich), and then (after you are prosperous) Rodney Lewis Boyd will have (in my possession) success (achievement, hit, accomplishment).*
> ~Joshua 1:8 with emphasis,
> additions, commentary mine, Ruminator Style

NOTE: Prosperity is having enough to meet your needs (not your greed) and an overflow to help others. Success is accomplishing the purposes of God in your life.

LOVE: agapaō (*ag-ap-ah'-o*)=Perhaps from ἄγαν agan (*much*); to *love* (in a social or moral sense): - (be-) love (-ed).

NOTE: *Love* is the great motivator. (Mark 12:28-34, James 2:8, John 3:16, John 13:34)

MANIFEST: emphanizō (*em-fan-id'-*)=From G1717; to *exhibit* (in person) or *disclose* (by words): - appear, declare (plainly), inform, (will) manifest, shew, signify. **G117: emphanēs** *(em-fan-ace')*= *apparent in self*: - manifest, openly.

NOTE: *Manifestation* is the great *revelation* of God Himself. (Exodus 33:18, Pro-Verbs 8:17)

When you walk in *full disclosure* you are walking in God's

open-door policy. When you are walking in obedience to the commandments you want to walk in wisdom.

> *Yet we do speak wisdom among those who are mature a wisdom, however* **NOT OF THIS AGE** *nor of the rulers* **OF THIS AGE** *who are passing away;* **BUT** *we speak God's wisdom which God predestined before the ages to our glory; the wisdom which none of the rulers of this age has understood; for if they had understood it they would not have crucified the Lord of glory;* **BUT** *just as it is written (in Isaiah 64:4, Isaiah 65:17), 'Things which eye has not seen and ear has not heard, and which have not entered the heart of man, all that God has prepared for those who love Him.'*
> ~1 Corinthians 2:6–9, emphasis and additions mine

> *"Wisdom is the principal thing; therefore get wisdom: and in all your getting get understanding."*
> ~Pro-Verbs 4:7

NOTE: We are talking about disclosure, revelations, manifestation of wisdom. The question is *how we get* this disclosure, revelation, manifestation (of Jesus, the ultimate wisdom). Of course, we have seen that it comes from having His commandments and obeying them.

> *For to us (you and me) God **revealed** them* **THROUGH THE SPIRIT** *(the Holy Spirit); for the Spirit (Big S) searches all things, even the depths of God.*
> ~1 Corinthians 2:10, Romans 8:26–27
> emphasis and additions mine

NOTE: Revelation, disclosure, manifestation is by the Spirit of God (aka The Holy Spirit). But now the question is how does He connect with humans?

> *For who among men know the thoughts of a man except the spirit (little s) of the man which is in him? (Even so) the thoughts of God*

no one knows except the Spirit (Big S) of God.
~1 Corinthians 2:11, additions mine

NOTE: We are now talking about the Holy Spirit, the human spirit, and thoughts (from God to man).

NOTE TO THE NOTE: Humans are three-part beings. We *are* a spirit (pneuma), we *have* a soul (psuche/psych) and we *live* in body (soma). Each part is separate but works synergistically.

Now may the God of peace (wholeness, rest, no stress or anxiety) Himself sanctify (set you apart for a purpose) entirely; and may your spirit (pneuma) and soul (psuche/psych) and body (soma) be preserved complete, without blame at the coming of our Lord Jesus Christ.
~I Thessalonians 5:23, addition mine

1. spirit (pneuma): "The spirit (little s) of an (humans) is the lamp of the Lord." (Pro-Verbs 20:27) A lamp is a clay vessel with oil in it and a wick laid in it that when lit gives of light, intimacy, and dissipates the darkness. Within our body is this lamp that house oil (the Holy Spirit), gifts of the Spirit that flows, fruit of the Spirit that grows and the place where there is intimacy with God and communication with God.
2. soul (psuche/psych): This is the location of the mind (what we think), will (what we freely choose based on what we think) and our emotions (the barometer of the soul).
3. body (soma): This includes our physical being including our flesh, blood, bones, internal organs, our brain, central and peripheral nervous systems etc.

Now we have received **NOT** *the spirit (little s) of the world, but the Spirit (Big S) who is from God,* **SO** *(the reason) that we may* **KNOW** *the things freely given to us by God.*
~1 Corinthians 2:12, emphasis and additions mine

KNOW: eidō (*i'-do*)=A primary verb properly to *see* (literally or figuratively); by implication (in the perfect only) to *know*: - be aware, behold, X can (+ not tell), consider, (have) known (-ledge), look (on), perceive, see, be sure, tell, understand, wist, wot.

NOTE: One of the secrets to success is that we can not only *know,* *that we know, that we know,* that we *know* about things we encounter in our lives, we can actually *know* the Creator of the universe intimately by the Spirit (Big S) in our human spirit (little s).

> *...which things we also speak not in words taught by human wisdom, but in those taught by the Spirit combining spiritual* **THOUGHTS** *with spiritual* **WORDS**.
> ~1 Corinthians 2:13, emphasis mine

NOTE: The Holy Spirit is known as our Teacher. (John 14:26, Nehemiah 9:20, Matthew 10:19–20, Mark 13:11, Luke 12:12, 2 Timothy 3:16–17)

NOTE TO THE NOTE: In another lesson we will talk about Paradigms/Mindsets, what we habitually think, speak, and do on another lesson, which ties in with "combining spiritual thoughts with spiritual words which speak of disclosure, revelations, manifestation and understanding.

> *But a natural man does not accept the things of the Spirit of God, for they are foolishness to him; and he cannot understand them, because they are spiritually appraised.*
> ~1 Corinthians 2:14

FOOLISHNESS: mōria (*mo-ree'-ah)*=From G3474; *silliness,* that is, *absurdity:* - foolishness.

G3474: mōros (*mo-ros')*=; *dull* or *stupid* (as if *shut* up), that is, *heedless,* (morally) *blockhead,* (apparently) *absurd:* - fool (-ish, X -ishness).

NOTE: As you approach success, sometimes the things that you do will appear to be foolish in the eyes of man, especially when you are getting your wisdom from your relationship with the manifested Jesus in your life.

SPIRITUALLY: pneumatikōs (*pnyoo-mat-ik-oce'*)=Adverb from G4152; *non-physically*, that is, *divinely*, *figuratively:* - spiritually **G415: pneumatikos (*phyoo-mat-ik-os'*)**=From G4151; *non-carnal*, that is, (humanly) *ethereal* (as opposed to gross), or (daemoniacally) a *spirit* (concretely), or (divinely) *supernatural, regenerate, religious:* - spiritual.. **G4151: pneuma *pnyoo'-mah*=**From G4154; a *current* of air, that is, *breath* (*blast*) or a *breeze*; by analogy or figuratively a *spirit*, that is, (human) the rational *soul*, (by implication) *vital principle*, mental *disposition*, etc., or (superhuman) an *angel*, *daemon*, or (divine) God, Christ's *spirit*, the Holy *spirit:* - ghost, life, spirit (-ual, -ually), mind. **G4154: pneō (*pneh'-o)*=**A primary word; to *breathe* hard, that is, *breeze*: - blow.

APPRAISED/DISCERNED: anakrinō (*an-ak-ree'-no)*= properly to *scrutinize*, that is, (by implication) *investigate, interrogate, determine:* - ask, question, discern, examine, judge, search.

NOTE: The carnal man with the carnal nature cannot discern/appraise spiritual things because we are talking spirit (little s) and Spirit (big S). You can only keep spiritual commandments by spiritual understanding. Walk and live by faith and Spirit for true success.

PRIORITIZE YOUR LOVE

But I have this against you, that you have left your first love. Therefore, remember from where you have fallen, and repent and do the deeds you did at first…"

~Revelation 2:4–5

"I love hot dogs, I love my wife, I love my dog, not necessarily in that order."

~Rodney Lewis Boyd

In the English language, there is only one word for the word love and that word is love; in the Greek language there are multiple words for the concept of love.

LOVE WORDS

1. Phileo: This word is where we get the word Philadelphia, the city of brother love. It is a Love that expresses emotion for other human beings.
2. Storgé: This word is for familial/family love or the love for a child, deep affection
3. Eros: This love is a sensual love that can entail sexual love. I can have eros for hotdogs or I have eros for my wife. When eros is defiled, it turns into lust because it is always taking.
4. Agapé: This is the God type of love, a giving love with no expectation of returned love.

In Napoleon Hill's book *Think and Grow Rich*, Chapter 11 is called

"The Mystery of Sex Transmutation. This is The Tenth Step Towards Riches." Transmutation is just an old word for change.

"The changing, or transferring of one element, or form of energy into another."

"Sexuality is such a strong emotion that it can effectively derail a pursuit of success."

"Sex transmutation is simple and easily explained. It means the switching of the mind from thoughts of physical expression to thoughts of some other nature."

The Mystery of Sex Transmutation
~Napoleon Hill

I believe misplaced love turns into lust, and we become open to temptation. Temptation is normally defined as "pulling you in/enticing you to some evil thing." But I believe a better definition is, "pulling you AWAY from who you really are and/or your purpose and destiny." It is a big distraction.

All of these loves, in themselves, are good and useful, but, when they are control by the God kind of love, agapé they function in a proper way.

But God demonstrates His own love (agapé) towards us in that while we were yet sinners, Christ died for us.
~Romans 5:8

a. What did God demonstrate? (Romans 5:8)
b. In what/who direction was this demonstration directed to? (Romans 5:8)
c. What were we "yet"? (Romans 5:8)
d. What did Christ (Jesus) do for us while we were "yet sinners"? (Romans 5:8)

I love this verse. It speaks of a demonstration, showing us how to do it. I think of someone demonstrating how to use cookware, knives, etc. God demonstrates how to love the unlovable. The way that I love is to wait for the sinner to clean up their own lives before

I give out my love to them. When I do this, I become a Go-Giver. When I do what God demonstrated and give out my love to someone before the deserved it (they never will be able to deserve it) I become a Go-Getter.

> *For God loved (agapé) the world that He gave His only begotten Son that whosever believes (trusts in, clings to, relies on, adheres to, cleaves to) in Him should not perish but have everlasting life."*
>
> ~John 3:16 addition mine

e. Who did God love? (John 3:16)

f. What did God give as a result of His love? (John 3:16)

g. What do we have to do to experience everlasting/eternal life? (John 3:16)

John 3:16 is also known as the central verse of the Bible that ties together the Old Testament (Old Covenant) and the New Testament (New Covenant) where Jesus fulfilled (not did away) the Law. The Father was a Go-Giver as He gave away His most precious and unique Son. The cause and effect were a harvest of sons and daughters. Imagine God not giving out the seed of His Son to the world. If you think the world is screwed up now, just imagine if God was a Go-Getter instead of being a Go-Giver.

> *A new commandment I give unto you, love (agapé) one another as I have loved (agapé) you, so you must love (agapé) one another.*
>
> ~John 13:34 addition mine

The old commandment was an eye for an eye, a tooth for a tooth. Once again, the standard for how to love was demonstrated by Christ. (The heart is the core of who we are. In the physical, the heart is the pump that circulates blood through the body for life. (Matthew 5:17–48) I like it when Jesus says, "But I say to you…".

h. What did Jesus give his followers? (John 13:34)

i. What was the old commandment? (Matthew 5:17–48, Leviticus 24:19-21)

j. What was the "new commandment" that Jesus gave us? (John 13:34)

This thing called prioritized love is directional. First it is towards the Lord our God. We love the Lord our God with all of our:

1. hearts
2. souls
3. mind
4. strength

which encompasses our entire being, loving God. Second our love must be towards ourselves. If you can't love and respect yourself, you can't love anyone else. Thirdly, we love our neighbors as we love ourselves. (Matthew 22:37–40, Mark 12:29–34)

k. Where is our love directed? (Mark 12:30)

l. What do we love the Lord with and how much of it do we do? (Mark 12:30)

Love the Lord your God with **ALL** your
and with **ALL** your
and with ALL your
and with **ALL** your
The second is this, You shall love your
as you love

~Mark 12:30–31

THE LOVE DEMONSTRATION

*But God demonstrates His own love toward us in that while we were **YET** sinners, Christ died for us.*

~Romans 5:8 emphasis mine

l. What direction is God's love toward? (Romans 5:8)

m. When was God's love directed towards us? (Romans 5:8)

n. When did Christ die for us? (Romans 5:8)

NOTE: How will you implement the demonstration that God gave about how to love and die for others? (Romans 5:8)

LOVE DEFINED (1 Corinthians 13:1–13)

o. What can you speak with and not have love? (1 Corinthians 13:1
NOTE: This letter of correction is speaking about the attitude that we should have when we speak in tongues of either men or angels. Again, it is not a letter of cessation, but correction.

p. What kind of noise do you make when you speak in tongues without love? (1 Corinthians 13:1)

q. What are you if you have the gift of prophecy, and know all mysteries and all knowledge; and have all mountain moving faith BUT do not love? (1 Corinthians 13:2)

r. What does it profit you if you give all of your possessions to feed the poor; and if you deliver your body to be burned, but do not have love? (1 Corinthians 13:3)

NOTE: 1 Corinthians 13:4–8 is the definitive definition of this thing called Agapé Love, the God type of love (versus Phileo (brotherly love) Storge' (familial love) and Eros (sensual love). When all of these loves are under control of Agapé Love then you begin to see.

*For God so **LOVED** that He gave His only begotten/unique Son, that whosoever (open to all) believes (trusts in, clings to, relies on, adheres to, cleaves to) in Him shall not perish but have everlasting life.*
~John 3:16 addition and emphasis mine

NOTE: Agapé love is the motivation for giving a valued thing for others.

LOVE: agapē (*ag-ah'-pay*)=From G25; *love*, that is, *affection* or *benevolence*; specifically (plural) a *love feast*: - (feast of) charity ([-ably]), dear, love. **G25: agapaō (*ag-ap-ah'-o*)**=Perhaps from ἀγαν agan (*much*; or compare [H5689]); to *love* (in a social or moral sense): - (be-) love (-ed).

1. Love is patient

PATIENT: makrothumeō (*mak-roth-oo-meh'-o)*= to *be long spir-ited*, that is, (objectively) *forbearing* or (subjectively) *patient:* - bear (suffer) long, be longsuffering, have (long) patience, be patient, patiently endure.

2. Love is kind

KIND: chrēsteuomai (*khraste-yoo'-om-ahee)*= to *show oneself useful*, that is, *act benevolently:* - be kind.

3. Love is not jealous

JEALOUS/ENVIOUS: zēloō (*dzay-lo'-o)*=From G2205; to *have warmth* of feeling for or against: - affect, covet (earnestly), (have) desire, (move with) envy, be jealous over, (be) zealous (-ly affect). G2205: zēlos (*dzay'-los)*= properly *heat*, that is, (figuratively) "zeal" (in a favorable sense, *ardor*; in an unfavorable one, *jealousy*, as of a husband [figuratively of God], or an enemy, *malice*): - emulation, envy (-ing), fervent mind, indignation, jealousy, zeal.

4. Love does not brag

BRAG/BOAST: Perpereuomai (*per-per-yoo'-om-ahee)*=Middle voice from πέρπερος perperos (*braggart*; to *boast:* - vaunt itself.

5. Love is not arrogant

ARROGANT: phusioō (*foo-see-o'-o)*=From G5449 in the pri-mary sense of *blowing*; to *inflate*, that is, (figuratively) *make proud* (*haughty*): - puff up. **G5449: phusis** (*foo'-sis)* =From G5453; *growth* (by *germination* or *expansion*), that is, (by implication) natural *production* (lineal *descent*); by extension a *genus* or *sort*; figuratively native *disposition, constitution* or *usage:* - ([man-]) kind, nature ([-al]). **G5453: phuō** (*foo'-o)*=A primary verb; probably originally to "puff" or *blow*, that is, to *swell* up; but only used in the implied sense, to *germinate* or *grow* (*sprout*, *produce*), literally or figuratively: - spring (up).

PUFFED UP: *phusioō (foo-see-o'-o)*=From G5449 in the primary sense of *blowing*; to *inflate*, that is, (figuratively) *make proud* (*haughty*): - puff up. **G5449: phusis (*foo'-sis)*=**From G5453; *growth* (by *germination* or *expansion*), that is, (by implication) natural *production* (lineal *descent*); by extension a *genus* or *sort*; figuratively native *disposition*, *constitution* or *usage:* - ([man-]) kind, nature ([-al]). **G5453: phuō (*foo'-o)*=**A primary verb; probably originally to "puff" or *blow*, that is, to *swell* up; but only used in the implied sense, to *germinate* or *grow* (*sprout*, *produce*), literally or figuratively: - spring (up).

6. Love does not act unbecomingly

UNSEEMINGLY/aschēmoneō (*as-kay-mon-eh'-o)*=From G809; to *be* (that is, *act*) *unbecoming:* - behave self-uncomely (unseemly). **G809: aschēmōn=*as-kay'-mone*=**properly *shapeless*, that is, (figuratively) *inelegant:* - uncomely.

7. Love does not seek its own

SEEK: zēteō (*dzay-teh'-o)*=Of uncertain affinity; to *seek* (literally or figuratively); specifically (by Hebraism) to *worship* (God), or (in a bad sense) to *plot* (against life): - be (go) about, desire, endeavor, enquire (for), require, (X will) seek (after, for, means).

OWN: heautou (*heh-ow-too')*=(Including all the other cases); from a reflexive pronoun otherwise obsolete and the genitive (dative or accusative) of G846; *him* (*her*, *it*, *them*, also [in conjunction with the personal pronoun of the other persons] *my*, *thy*, *our*, *your*) -self (-selves), etc.: - alone, her (own, -self), (he) himself, his (own), itself, one (to) another, our (thine) own (-selves), + that she had, their (own, own selves), (of) them (-selves), they, thyself, you, your (own, own conceits, own selves, -selves).

8. Love is not provoked

PROVOKED: paroxunō (*par-ox-oo'-no*)= to *sharpen alongside*, that is, (figuratively) to *exasperate:* - easily provoke, stir.

9. Love does not take into account a wrong suffered

EASILY PROVOKED/TAKE INTO ACCOUNT A WRONG SUFFERED: paroxunō (*par-ox-oo'-no*)= to *sharpen alongside*, that is, (figuratively) to *exasperate:* - easily provoke, stir.

EVIL: kakos (*kak-os'*)=Apparently a primary word; *worthless* (*intrinsically* such; that is, (subjectively) *depraved*, or (objectively) *injurious:* - bad, evil, harm, ill, noisome, wicked.

10. Love does not rejoice in unrighteousness

REJOICE: chairō (*khah'ee-ro*)=A primary verb; to be full of *"cheer,"* that is, calmly *happy* or well off; impersonal especially as a salutation (on meeting or parting), *be well:* - farewell, be glad, God speed, greeting, hail, joy (-fully), rejoice.

UNRIGHTEOUSNESS: adikia (*ad-ee-kee'-ah*)=From G94; (legal) *injustice* (properly the quality, by implication the act); moral *wrongfulness* (of character, life or act): - iniquity, unjust, unrighteousness, wrong. **G94: adikos(*ad'-ee-kos*unjust:** by extension *wicked*; by implication *treacherous*; specifically *heathen:* - unjust, unrighteous.

11. Love rejoices with the truth

REJOICE: chairō (*khah'ee-ro*)=A primary verb; to be full of *"cheer,"* that is, calmly *happy* or well off; impersonal especially as a salutation (on meeting or parting), *be well:* - farewell, be glad, God speed, greeting, hail, joy (-fully), rejoice.

TRUTH: alētheia (*al-ay'-thi-a*)=From G227; *truth:* - true, X truly, truth, verity. **G227: alēthēs** *(=al-ay-thace')= true* (as *not concealing*): - true, truly, truth.

12. Love bears all things

BEARS: stegō *(steg'-o)=*From G4721; to *roof* over, that is, (figuratively) to *cover* with silence (*endure* patiently): - (for-) bear, suffer. **G4721: stegē** *(steg'-ay)=*Strengthened from a primary word τέγος tegos (a "thatch" or "deck" of building); a *roof:* - roof.

THINGS: pas *(pas)=*Including all the forms of declension; apparently a primary word; *all, any, every,* the *whole:* - all (manner of, means) alway (-s), any (one), X daily, + ever, every (one, way), as many as, + no (-thing), X throughly, whatsoever, whole, whosoever.

13. Love believes all things

BELIEVE: pisteuō *(pist-yoo'-o)=*From G4102; to *have faith* (in, upon, or with respect to, a person or thing), that is, *credit*; by implication to *entrust* (especially one's spiritual wellbeing to Christ): - believe (-r), commit (to trust), put in trust with. **G4102: pistis** *(pis'-tis)=*From G3982; *persuasion*, that is, *credence*; moral *conviction* (of *religious* truth, or the truthfulness of God or a religious teacher), especially *reliance* upon Christ for salvation; abstractly *constancy* in such profession; by extension the system of religious (Gospel) *truth* itself: - assurance, belief, believe, faith, fidelity. **G3982: peithō** *(pi'-tho)=*A primary verb; to *convince* (by argument, true or false); by analogy to *pacify* or *conciliate* (by other fair means); reflexively or passively to *assent* (to evidence or authority), to *rely* (by inward certainty): - agree, assure, believe, have confidence, be (wax) content, make friend, obey, persuade, trust, yield.

THINGS: pas *(pas)=*Including all the forms of declension; apparently a primary word; *all, any, every,* the *whole:* - all (manner of, means) alway (-s), any (one), X daily, + ever, every (one, way), as many as, + no (-thing), X throughly, whatsoever, whole, whosoever.

14. Love hopes all things

HOPES: elpizō (*el-pid'-zo*)=From G1680; to *expect* or *confide:* - (have, thing) hope (-d) (for), trust. **G1680: elpis (*el-pece'*)**=From ἔλπω elpō which is a primary word (to *anticipate*, usually with pleasure); *expectation* (abstract or concrete) or *confidence:* - faith, hope. (Confident expectation

THINGS: pas (*pas*)=Including all the forms of declension; apparently a primary word; *all*, *any*, *every*, the *whole:* - all (manner of, means) alway (-s), any (one), X daily, + ever, every (one, way), as many as, + no (-thing), X throughly, whatsoever, whole, whosoever.

15. Love endures all things

ENDURES: hupomenō=*hoop-om-en'-o*= to *stay under* (*behind*), that is, *remain*; figuratively to *undergo*, that is, *bear* (trials), *have fortitude*, *persevere:* - abide, endure, (take) patient (-ly), suffer, tarry behind.

THINGS: pas (*pas*)=Including all the forms of declension; apparently a primary word; *all*, *any*, *every*, the *whole:* - all (manner of, means) alway (-s), any (one), X daily, + ever, every (one, way), as many as, + no (-thing), X throughly, whatsoever, whole, whosoever.

16. Love never fails

LOVE: agapē (*ag-ah'-pay*)=From G25; *love*, that is, *affection* or *benevolence*; specifically (plural) a *love feast:* - (feast of) charity ([-ably]), dear, love. **G25: agapaō (*ag-ap-ah'-o*)**=Perhaps from ἄγαν agan (*much*; or compare [H5689]); to *love* (in a social or moral sense): - (be-) love (-ed).

NEVER: oudepote (*oo-dep'-ot-eh*=)*not even at any time*, that is, *never at all:* - neither at any time, never, nothing at any time.

FAILS: katargeō (*kat-arg-eh'-o*)= to *be* (render) *entirely idle* (*useless*), literally or figuratively: - abolish, cease, cumber, deliver, destroy, do away, become (make) of no (none, without) effect, fail, loose, bring (come) to nought, put away (down), vanish away, make void.

NOTE: When you prioritize true agapé love, your priorities change from selfish love to giving love. True love is more than an emotion. Yes, love is an emotion, but it is not a selfish lust that fluctuates with the emotional climate.

DISCOVER THE SECRETS OF THE SEED/SOIL

Now He who supplies seed to the sower and bread for good will supply and multiply your seed for sowing and increase the harvest of your righteousness.

~2 Corinthians 9:10

$\mathbf{A}$s we journey on the road to success, we need to realize that God is on our side and even *supplies* what we need for *strength* and *supply* that is needed for success. He is the Seed Supplier for Sowing to Success.

I have strength (forte, power, intensity) for all things in Christ Who empowers me [I am ready for anything and equal to anything through Him Who infuses inner strength into me; I am self-sufficient in Christ's sufficiency.

~Philippians 4:13 Amplified Bible)

NOTE: Philippians 4:13 is in the context of money.

And my God will liberally (copiously, generously, freely) supply (source, provision, stock) (fill to the full) your every need (essentials, demand) according to His riches in glory in Christ Jesus.

~Philippians 4:19 Amplified Bible

NOTE: There is not a shortage of supply in "His riches in glory/ His presence" or in His Anointing (Christ).

SEED: Sperma (*sper'-mah*)=From G4687; something *sown*, that is, *seed* (including the male "sperm"); by implication *offspring*; specifically, a *remnant* (figuratively as if kept over for planting): - issue, seed. **G4687: speirō** (*spi'-ro)*=Probably strengthened from G4685 (through the idea of *extending*); to *scatter*, that is, *sow* (literally or figuratively): - sow (-er), receive seed.

SEED: (1) the grains of ripened ovules of plants used for sowing (2) the fertilized ripened ovule of a flowering plant containing an embryo and capable normally of germination to produce a new plant (Meriam-Webster Dictionary)

A seed whether in human form or horticultural form contains the DNA to reproduce what is in that seed. The bottom line is that in the original form, the seed is from God for a purpose.

In the Gospel of Mark, we see Jesus the Teacher, teaching about the Kingdom (rule, reign, realm, foundation of power) of God using imagery and parables of seed (the Word), soil (the hearts) and sowers (people who broadcast seed/Word). (Mark 4:1–20, Luke 8:4–15, Matthew 13:1–23) The seed/the Word is sown (broadcast, flung out by the handful) and lands on the soil, no matter what the condition of the soil is. As powerful as the seed/Word is (it will endure forever, 1 Peter 1:25, Matthew 24:35, Isaiah 40:8), when it is received in the soil/heart, if the heart is not a good heart/good soil the seed is in danger from birds/satan, rocky soil with no depth for roots and scorching sun and withers away, thorns choking it destroying the seed and the productivity of the seed. (Mark 4: 3–8) The birds, no depth, thorns represent satan, affliction, persecution, worries of the world, the deceitful of riches, and desires for other things makes the seed/the Word of none effect in the life of people.

NOTE: Many people use the phrase, "the heart wants what it wants or else it does not care." (Emily Dickenson, 1862 from a letter by Ms. Dickenson). When people are just "following their hearts" the could be going astray according to Jeremiah 17: 9.

The heart is more deceitful than all else and it is desperately sick;

who can understand it.

~Jeremiah 17:9

*Then I will sprinkle clean water on you, and you will be clean; I will cleanse you from all your filthiness and from all your idles **AND** I will give you a new heart and put a new spirit within you; and I will remove the heart of stone from your flesh and give you a heart of flesh. And I will put My Spirit within you and cause you to walk in My statues, and you will be careful to observe my ordinances."*

~Ezekiel 36:25–27 emphasis mine

You can't trust an old heart just like the ways and thoughts of the wicked and unrighteous men are not His ways and thoughts (but believers have the mind of Christ, the ways and thoughts of God). (Isaiah 55:6–7, Isaiah 55:8–9, 1 Corinthians 2:9–16)

So, think (like God thinks) of money as seed and the business as soil. Sow the seed into the soil, sow the money into the business, **BUT** make sure the soil is *good soil*, void of rocks, thorns/weeds/birds snatching the seed out of the soil. Make sure the soil is weeded, fertilized, watered, etc., **IF** you want a prosperous and successful harvest at various rates of return (30, 60, 100-Fold)

One of the great *secrets of the seed* is *caring for the soil*. Another great secret of the seed is being careful what kind of seed you are planting in the soil of the heart. It has been said by many people, "the soil is no respecter of the seed, it will produce whatever is plant." It does not matter if you plant corn, okra, tomatoes, nightshade, poison ivy or kudzu. They will grow.

RODFUCIOUS SAYS: "Man who plants seeds of poison ivy should not be surprised when he reaps a harvest of rash and itching."

Now He who supplies seed to the sower and bread for good will supply and multiply your seed for sowing and increase the harvest of your righteousness.

~2 Corinthians 9:10

Is the supplier of the seed supplying it for good or bad? According to 2 Corinthians 9:10:

1. God supplies the seed
2. The seed is supplied to the sower (for the purpose of sowing)
3. The seed sown is for the good, not the bad
4. The supplied seed is for multiplication of the seed for more sowing (one corn seed produces a stalk of corn with multiple ears of corn that has multiple kernels of corn.
5. The seed is meant to increase (in harvest and in the spiritual, your righteousness right standing.

> *And I (Jesus) assure you, most solemnly I tell you, unless a grain (seed) of wheat falls into the earth and dies, it remains [just one] grain/seed; it never becomes more but lives] by itself alone]. But (in contrast) if it dies, it produces many others and yields a rich harvest.*
> ~John 12:24 Amplified Bible with additions, emphasis, and commentary mine, Ruminator Style

Of course, Jesus is referring to Himself as the Seed that must die (on the cross) and be buried in the tomb so that He can be resurrected and produce not just one, only, begotten Son, but would produce multiple sons and daughters IF they believe (trust in, cling to, rely on, adhere to, cleave to) Him and the D.B.R., Death, Burial and Resurrection.

> *The Kingdom of God is like a man who scatters seed upon the ground, and then continues sleeping and rising night and day while the seed sprouts and grows and increases—he knowns not how. The earth produces [acting by itself]—first the blade, then the ear, then the full grain in the ear. But when the grain is ripe and permits, immediately he sends forth (the reapers] and puts in the sickle, because the harvest stands ready.*
> ~Mark 4:26–29 additiona mine

I like the orderly progression of growth and harvest, with the cause and effect being harvest of what was sown, good, bad, or ugly.

Do not be deceived and deluded and misled; God will not allow Himself to be sneered at (scorned, disdained, or mocked by mere professions, or by His precepts (principles/laws) being set aside. [He inevitably deludes himself who attempts to delude God.] For whatever (good, bad or ugly) a man (woman, human) sows that and that only is what he will reap.

~Galatians 6:7 Amplified Bible with emphasis, additions, and commentary mine, Ruminator Style

Once again, we are talking about the cause and effect of sowing and reaping. Seed can be good seed, bad seed or ugly seed and the harvest will be determined by soil type. Of course, the spiritual principle can also be applied to business principles, personal principles.

For he who sows to his own flesh (lower nature, sensuality) will from the flesh reap decay and ruin and destruction, but he who sows to the Spirit will from the Spirit reap eternal life.

~Galatians 6:8 Amplified Bible

The soil can either be bad soil or good soil. The spiritual soil can be flesh (carnality) or the soil can be Spirit (spiritual). Add bad seed to bad soil get bad harvest and add good seed to good soil get good harvest.

In the morning sow your seed and in the evening withhold not your hands, for you know not your hands, for you know not which that prosper/succeed, whether this or that or whether both alike will be good.

~Ecclesiastes 11:6

The bottom-line is don't give up on the seed morning or night, it is producing and will succeed and prosper eventually.

While the earth remains, seedtime and harvest, cold and heat, summer and winter, and day and night shall not cease.

~Genesis 8:22

The natural law/principle of nature (set into motion by the Creator of nature) goes on and on and on. As long as we tap into the natural of the Supernatural God, we will reap and have harvest in the cycle of life.

One last thought on the secrets of the seed, or the secrets of investing in financial and personal affairs, once you plant the seed, don't go immediately and dig up the seed to see if it is doing what the seed does, grow. Many times we plant seeds of faith with our thoughts and our words and our actions, but in doubt, when we dig up the seed and we experience failure instead of success. This results in crop failure.

SOIL TYPES (Mark 4:1–20, Luke 8:4–15, Matthew 13:1–23)

In these parables of the Kingdom, the one constant is the **SEED**. The Seed is the Word of God sown into the various soils. As powerful was the Seed/Word of God is, it can be stolen (by satan), scorched (by persecutions and afflictions), and choked out (by the worries of the world, the deceitfulness of riches, and desires for other things). This goes along with how powerful the Word/Seed is, it can be made of none effect, ineffectual by the traditions of men that nullify the Word. (Mark 7:13) The soil types are:

1. Beside the road
2. Rocky ground
3. Among the thorns
4. Good soil.

And the seed (the Word) in the good soil, these are the ones who have heard the Word/Seed in an honest and good heart, and hold it fast, and bear fruit with perseverance.

~Luke 8:15 addition mine

Trust in the Lord and do good; dwell in the land and **CULTIVATE FAITHFULNESS** *(on your part and feed on the faithfulness of God).*

~Psalm 37:4 addition and emphasis mine

TO WANT OR NOT TO WANT?

*Not that I speak from want for I have **learned to be content** in whatever circumstances I am.*
                              ~Philippians 4:11, emphasis mine

O ne of the most important secrets to success is *speaking correctly*. There is power in the tongue for good or bad, positive, or negative, blessing or curse.

Death and life are in the power of the tongue, and they who indulge in it shall eat the fruit of it [for death or evil].
                              ~Pro-Verbs 18:21, addition mine

The power (exousia=delegated authority and dunamis= dynamic, miracle ability) to choose what you speak will determine what you allow into your life. The tongue represents the thoughts expressed. Close your eyes and see a closed door and you bend down and put the doorknob in your mouth and turn your head and open the door. That is a wild and crazy image, but it represents the fact that we open the door of good, bad, ugly, blessing, curse, prosperity, poverty, success, and failure **BY OUR MOUTHS**, what we think and then express out loud.

*As a man **thinketh** in his heart/mind, so he is.*
                              ~Pro-Verbs 23:7 emphasis mine

Thinking is not just a casual thought, but it is what *you dwell on,* what *you focus on*, what *you imagine about*. **IF** you constantly think that you can never make a sell, guess what, you will never make a sell. **IF** you constantly think about failure, you will be a failure. **IF** you constantly think about success, you will be a success. Of course, just thinking it does not mean it will happen but when you begin to act based on what you think, then you open the door to whatever you are thinking.

> *...out of the abundance (overflow) of the heart/mind, **the mouth speaks**.*"
>
> ~Luke 6:45 addition and emphasis mine

The mouth is the *great revealer of your thoughts*. The saying is, "Where your dwelling, will be telling." That simply means that your mouth will speak what you're thinking. As Zig Ziglar the great motivator says, "Many have stinking thinking." Stinking thinking leads to stinking speaking." Many have *"halitosis of the mind,"* stinking thoughts. Many have "Lazarus Breath," after three days your thoughts and your words "stinketh."

Bad breath is not just a mouth thing. "The tongue is the mirror of the colon." When you go to bed at night and wake up in the morning, there is a film on the tongue, aka a morning mouth that has a Lazarus smell, "he stinketh." (John 11:39) The toxins of the colon are revealed in the mouth. So, it is with what we think, overflowing out of our mouth.

We need to practice speaking like God speaks.

> *As it is written, I (God) have made you (Abraham) the father of many nations (Covenant Promise). He (Abraham) was appointed our father] in the sight of God in Whom he (Abraham) believed (trusted in, clung to, relied on, adhered to, cleaved to), Who (God) gives life to the dead and **speaks** of the non-existent things that [He (God) has foretold and promised] as IF they [already] existed.*
>
> ~Genesis 17:5, Romans 4:17 additions and emphasis mine

"We need to imitate God and call things that are **NOT** as

though they **WERE** instead of calling things that **ARE** as if they **WILL NEVER CHANGE**."

~Rodney Lewis Boyd

Faith (the substance of things hoped for, the evidence of things not seen, what you believe) **without corresponding actions** *(deeds, works, what you do)* is **of none effect** *(not effective, dead).*

~James 2:17 Weymouth Translation with emphasis, additions, and commentary mine, Ruminator Style

What you *think* and *speak* and what you *do* will determine the outcomes in your life. You can think about something, but nothing really happens until you speak it forth and nothing really happens unless you act upon what you think and speak, **BUT** however if you think negative and speak negative you attract negative and will most likely will be acted upon. Reverse engineer that and start thinking positive, speaking positive and doing positive and see what happens.

This lead us to the original verse and secret for success, Philippians 4:11.

*Not that **I speak** from want for I have **learned** to **be content** in whatever circumstances I am.*

Philippians 4:11, emphasis mine

Paul **DID NOT** speak (verbalize his thoughts) from a position of *want*. Remember, he was in a Roman prison for preaching the Gospel and surely *had needs*, however, he had learned a principle (*a secret*) of not speaking from a position of want. That does not mean that it is wrong to want, just not thinking and speaking from that position. I believe that what he learned was that *His God had everything that he needed and so he didn't have to want it, it was his*. King David had learned this same secret, as evidenced by, "The Lord is my Shepherd, I shall *NOT WANT*." (Psalm 23:1)

IF you are wanting, you may need to check out your relationship with the Shepherd.

NOT THAT I SPEAK

SPEAK: legō (*leg'-o*)=A primary verb; properly to "lay" forth, that is, (figuratively) *relate* (in words [usually of systematic or set *discourse*; whereas G2036 and G5346 generally refer to an *individual* expression or speech respectively; while G4483 is properly to *break silence* merely, and G2980 means an *extended* or random harangue]); by implication to *mean:* - ask, bid, boast, call, describe, give out, name, put forth, say (-ing, on), shew, speak, tell, utter.

WANT: husterēsis (*hoos-ter'-ay-sis*)=From G5302; a *falling short*, that is, (specifically) *penury:* - want. **G5302: hustereō (*hoos-ter-eh'-o*)**=From G5306; to *be later*, that is, (by implication) to *be inferior*; genitively to *fall short* (*be deficient*): - come behind (short), be destitute, fall, lack, suffer need, (be in) want, be the worse. **G5306: husteros (*hoos'-ter-os-)*=Comparatively from G5259 (in the sense of *behind*); *later:* - latter.

LEARNED: manthanō (*man-than'-o*)=Prolonged from a primary verb, another form of which, μαθέω matheō, is used as an alternate in certain tenses; to *learn* (in any way): - learn, understand.

STATE: The particular condition that someone or something is in at a specific time.

CONTENT: autarkēs (*ow-tar'-kace*)= *self complacent (smug or uncritical satisfaction), that is, contented (in a state of peaceful happiness, a state of satisfaction):* - content.

The secret to success when you are faced with lack is to come into the understanding that no matter what you *do have or don't have,* that in whatever circumstances, situation, trouble, trial that you are facing, that:

> **"I CAN DO** all things through Christ (the Anointed One and His anointing) who strengthens (infuses you with strength) me."
> ~Philippians 4:13, emphasis and addition mine

That includes living with:
1. Humble means
2. In prosperity
3. Being filled
4. Going hungry
5. Having abundance
6. Suffering need
7. Gas prices at $1.25
8. Gas prices at $4.75
9. Republicans in the White House
10. Democrats in the White House
11. When life is fair
12. When life sucks
13. (fill in the blank of when things are good, bad or ugly)

And my God will liberally supply (fill to the full) your every need according to His riches in glory in Christ Jesus.
~Philippians 4:19, Amplified Bible

THE WEALTH MAKER

But you shall remember the Lord your God, for it is He Who is
giving you power *(control, ability)* **to make wealth.**
~Deuteronomy 8:18, emphasis and addition mine

As long as you think that it is God's will for you to be poor and to be under the thumb of poverty, you will never be *prosperous* or a success. As long as you are convinced that wealth is of the d-evil and the plot of capitalistic agenda to keep certain people down and others up then you will always live in an us and them mentality.

The d-evil (the evil one, the liar, the father of lies, the thief, the stealer, killer, destroyer, the tempter) does not want us to remember (to have a memory loss) that it is God who is giving you the "power to make wealth." In the book of Deuteronomy, the provisions and ratification of the Covenant of God that God had made with Abraham and the Children of Israel are laid out. (Deuteronomy 27–29)

I call heaven and earth to witness against you today, that I have set before you life and death, the blessing and the curse. So, **CHOOSE LIFE** *in order that you may live, you and your descendants, by loving the Lord your God, by obeying His voice, and by holding fast to Him; for this is your life and the length of your days, that you may live in the land which the Lord swore to your fathers, to Abraham, Isaac, and Jacob to give them.*

~Deuteronomy 30:19

The access into these blessings, this position of wealth, is via the portal of a tree.

> *For as many as are of the works of the Law are under a curse;*
> *for it is written cursed I everyone who does not abide by all things*
> *written in the book of the law, to perform them.*
> ~Galatians 3:10, Deuteronomy 27:26

> *Now that no one is justified by the Law before God is evident;*
> *for the righteous man shall live by faith.*
> ~Galatians 3:11, Habakkuk 2:4,
> Romans 1:17, Hebrews 10:38

> *However, the Law is not of faith; on the contrary, he who practices*
> *them shall live by them.*
> ~Galatians 3:12, Leviticus 18:5

> *Christ (Jesus, the Anointed One who was anointed with yoke*
> *breaking, burden lifting, oppression removing, healing power of the*
> *Holy Ghost)* **REDEEMED US** *(bought us, became the propitiation,*
> *the satisfactory substitute) from the curse.*
> ~Galatians 3:13, Acts 10:38, I John 2:2,
> Deuteronomy 21:23, addition and emphasis mine

> *In order that* **IN CHRIST JESUS** *the* **BLESSINGS OF**
> **ABRAHAM** *might come to the gentiles (non-covenant people), so*
> *that we would receive the promise of the Spirit through faith.*
> Galatians 3:13, Deuteronomy 28:1–14,
> addition and emphasis mine

> *Now it shall be, if you will diligently obey the Lord, you God,*
> *being careful to do all His commandments which I command you*
> *today, the Lord your God will set you high above all the nations of*
> *the earth. All these* **BLESSINGS** *shall come upon you and overtake*
> *you if you obey the Lord your God.*
> ~Deuteronomy 28:1–2, emphasis mine

NOTE: The obedience is found in John 14:21:

He (you) who has My (Jesus) commandments and keeps them, he (you) it is who loves Me (Jesus) and he (you) who loves Me (Jesus) will be loved by My (Jesus) Father (who art in heaven) and I (Jesus) will love him(you) and will manifest, disclose, reveal Myself (Jesus) to him (you).

~John 14:21, with emphasis, additions, commentary by me Ruminator Style

Once again, the will of God is not poverty but wealth and not only that, but He also gave us the power to make wealth. This is also known as, blessing. When people take a "vow of poverty" they are taking a "vow of a curse." Here are a few things available for us when we are walking in the **BLESSINGS** (because of Jesus in our lives):

1. Led in the wilderness (here on earth until he returns)
2. Fed with manna (provision)
3. Live by everything that comes from the mouth of God (words/breath/Spirit)
4. Longevity of clothing
5. No foot swelling
6. Brought into good land
7. A land of brooks of water of fountains and springs flowing forth in valleys and hills
8. A land of wheat, barley, vines, figs, pomegranates, olive oil, honey
9. A land where you shall eat food without scarcity
10. You shall not lack anything
11. A land whose stones are iron and out of whose hills you can dig copper
12. Eat with satisfaction
13. Bless/thank/be grateful to the Lord for provision, built houses, living in them, herds and flocks multiplied, silver and gold
14. We will be led through the wilderness with its fiery, scorpions, thirsty ground with no water (He brought water for you out of the rock of flint)

15. We will eat and be satisfied

16. We will bless the Lord for the land He has given us

The bottom line is this, what God did for the children of Israel and because of Jesus we tap into the **BLESSINGS OF ABRAHAM.** (Galatians 3:14)

> *But you shall remember the Lord your God, for it is He who is* ***GIVING YOU THE POWER TO MAKE WEALTH,*** *that He may confirm His covenant which he swore to your fathers, as it is this day.*
> ~Deuteronomy 8:18, emphasis mine

Does that sound like poverty and failure to you? Me neither. It sounds like prosperity and success.

> "I believe the secret lies in not what you have but what you do with what you have."
> ~Andrew Carnegie, *The Gospel of Wealth*

There are many people in the Old and Testament that were rich/wealthy including: Abraham , Isaac, Jacob, Job, Joseph and his brothers, Lot, Job, Boaz Abigail, Nabal, King David, Solomon Hezekiah, Zacchaeus, Matthew, Joseph of Arimathea, the Roman Centurion Lydia , Dorcas Barnabas, Philemon. Even Jesus' ministry had a treasury (a money bag/a money box) and treasurer—Judas. (John 13:29). There was enough money in the money box of Jesus' ministry that Judas would pilfer money from it. Judas even complained about wasted ointment that Mary poured on Jesus' feet could be sold for 300 denarii and given to poor people. (See John 12:1–8) No, Jesus was not a mega millionaire, but His Father had cattle on a thousand hills. (Psalm 50:10–12)

Throughout the New Testament we see people who had wealth but used their wealth for the Gospel which included:

1. Joseph called Barnabas (Acts 4: 36–37)

2. Dorcas (Acts 9:36)

3. Cornelius (Acts 10:1)

4. Sergius Paulus (Acts 13:6–12)
5. Lydia (Acts 16:14–150
6. Aquila and Priscilla (Acts 18:2–3)
7. Mnason of Cyprus (Acts 21:16)
8. Philemon (Philemon 1)

"Just as poverty doesn't guarantee virtue, wealth does not guarantee vice/greed."

~Unknown

DEAL WITH THE ROOT OF ALL KINDS OF EVIL

*For the love of money is **a root of all sorts of evil**, and some by longing for it have wandered away from the faith and pierced themselves with many griefs.*

> ~1 Timothy 6:10, emphasis mine

-What is the root of all sorts of evil? (1 Timothy 6:10)

-What happened to some (not all) who have longed for it? (1 Timothy 6:10)

-When they wandered from the faith, what did they pierce themselves with? (1Timothy 6:10)

One of the most misquoted verses in the Bible is 1 Timothy 6:10.

Money is the root of all sorts of evil, and some by longing for it (money) have wandered away from the faith and pierced themselves with many griefs.

> ~1 Timothy 6:10 misquoted

-How do people twist 1 Timothy 6:10?

-What is **NOT** the root of all sources of evil? (1 Timothy 6:10)

-What *IS* the root of all sources of evil? (1 Timothy 6:10)

The cause and effect is that "traditions of men" have invalidated and nullified the Word of God (Mark 7:13) concerning money, prosperity, and success.

The version of it is:

> For the **LOVE** of money is **A** (not the only one) root of **ALL** sorts of evil, and some by longing (lusting) for it have wandered away from the faith and pierced themselves with many griefs.
>
> ~1 Timothy 6:10 with emphasis, additions and commentary mine, Ruminator Style

-Is there just one root or many roots of evil? (1 Timothy 6:10)

LOVE OF MONEY: philarguria (*fil-ar-goo-ree'-ah*)=From G5366; *avarice:* - love of money. **G5366: philarguros** (*fil-ar'-goo-ros fond of silver* (*money*), that is, *avaricious:* - covetous.

AVARICE: Extreme greed for wealth or material gain

COVETOUS: Having or showing great desire to possess something belonging to someone else.

In our previous secret to success we saw that it was God who gave us the *power/ability to make wealth* and that *wealth was part of the Covenant Promise.* I don't believe that God gave us the power/ability to be held down by *the root of all kinds of evil.*

Before we get to 1 Timothy 6:10, let's take a look back at 1 Timothy 6:6–9 in reference to money.

> But **godliness** actually is a means of **great gain,** when accompanied with **contentment.**"
>
> **~1 Timothy 6:6**

-What do you think is better than money? (1 Timothy 6:6)

-What is needed for godliness to be great gain? (1 Timothy 6:6)

GODLINESS eusebeia (*yoo-seb'-i-ah)*=From G2152; *piety;* specifically the *gospel* scheme: - godliness, holiness. **G2152: eusebēs (*yoo-seb-ace')*=** *well reverent*, that is, *pious:* - devout, godly.

GAIN: porismos (*por-is-mos')*= (a *way*, that is, *means*); *furnishing (procuring)*, that is, (by implication) *money getting (acquisition):* - gain.

CONTENTMENT: Autarkeia (*ow-tar'-ki-ah)*=From G842; *self-satisfaction*, that is, (abstractly) *contentedness*, or (concretely) a *competence:* - contentment, sufficiency. **G842: autarkēs=*ow-tar'-kace;* *self-complacent*, that is, *contented:* - content.

It has been said that money can't buy happiness, but it can make misery a little more comfortable. I believe that money/wealth can coexist with happiness. This verse goes well with Pro-Verbs 10:22

> *The blessing of the Lord, it makes rich and adds no sorrow with it.*
> ~Pro-Verbs 10:20

-What does the "blessing of the Lord" make? (Pro-Verbs 10:22)

Reverse engineer that verse and it reads:

> *the curse of the d-evil makes poor/poverty and adds a boatload of sorrow with it.*
> ~Pro-Verbs 10:22 with emphasis, additions, and commentary mine, Ruminator Style

-What makes poor/poverty? (Pro-Verbs 10:22)

-What does poor/poverty by the curse of the d-evil add to us? (Pro-Verbs 10:22)

People scrape and fight, and hoard wealth as if they will take it with you, but there are no trailers being carried behind the hearse when we die.

For we have brought nothing (nada, zilch, zip, zero, nuttin' honey) into the world, so we cannot take anything out of it either."
~1 Timothy 6:7, addition mine

-What did we **NOT** bring into the world? (1 Timothy 6:7)

-What can we **NOT** take out of the world that we brought nothing into? (1 Timothy 6:7)

IF *we have food and covering, with these we shall be content.*
~1 Timothy 6:8, emphasis mine

This verse goes hand in hand with Jesus' teaching about the Kingdom of God in Matthew 6:25–34.

Therefore I say unto you, Take no thought for your life, what ye shall eat, or what ye shall drink; nor yet for your body, what ye shall put on. Is not the life more than meat, and the body than raiment?
~Matthew 6:25

-What are we to not take though about? (Matthew 6:25)

-What is life more than? (Matthew 6:25)

Behold the fowls of the air: for they sow not, neither do they reap, nor gather into barns; yet your heavenly Father feedeth them. Are ye not much better than they?
~Matthew 6:26

-What do the fowls of the Air **NOT** do? (Matthew 6:26)

Which of you by taking thought can add one cubit unto his stature?
~Matthew 6:27

-Can you add anything to you but taking thought? (Matthew 6:27)

And why take ye thought for raiment? Consider the lilies of the field, how they grow; they toil not, neither do they spin:

And yet I say unto you, That even Solomon in all his glory was not arrayed like one of these.

~Matthew 6:28, 29

-Should we take thought about our clothes? (Matthew 6:28)

-What three things do the lilies of the field NOT do? (Matthew 6:28)

-How do the lilies of the field compare to Solomon's clothes? (Matthew 6:28)

Wherefore, if God so clothe the grass of the field, which today is, and tomorrow is cast into the oven, shall he not much more clothe you, O ye of little faith?

~Matthew 6:30

-When we take thought about things like clothes, what is the size of our faith? (Matthew 6:30)

Therefore take no thought, saying, What shall we eat? or, What shall we drink? or, Wherewithal shall we be clothed?

(For after all these things do the Gentiles seek:) for your heavenly Father knoweth that ye have need of all these things.

~Matthew 6:31, 32

-What three things should we not take thought about? (Matthew 6:31)
1.
2.
3.

NOTE: These are all things for which we use money to purchase. **IF** we "lust" after money then we will be "lusting" after the things that we buy with that money and this "lust" will draw us away from our faith towards God and His Kingdom.

> *But seek ye first the kingdom of God, and his righteousness; and all these things shall be added unto you.*
>
> ~Matthew 6:33

-What two thing should we seek first if we want them to be added to us? (Matthew 6:33)

> *Take therefore no thought for the morrow: for the morrow shall take thought for the things of itself. Sufficient unto the day is the evil thereof.*
>
> ~Matthew 6:34

-What should we not take thought for and why? (Matthew 6:34)

LEARN TO THINK, SPEAK, AND DO

Here is some collective wisdom from the Bible about speaking and thinking and doing which will result in prosperity and success. Take some time, look up the verses and answer the questions. The secret is to think with a renewed mind, speak from a renewed mind and act based on what you think and speak.

THINK: "As a man *thinketh* in his heart/mind so he is." (Pro-Verbs 23:7)

-What makes you who you are? (Pro-Verbs 23:7)

-Where do you think? (Pro-Verbs 23:7)

Many think that their "thinker" is their brain, but it is not. The brain is in the body and is the physical switching station of nerve impulses.

A human's soul is his *mind* (what he thinks), his *will* (what he freely chooses based on what he thinks) and his *emotions* (the barometer of his feelings). When you *take control* of what you *think*, you will be more likely to *choose* wisely in what you speak and do, and then your emotions will be *regulated* instead of being out of control.

I am convinced that what we *habitually* think, habitually speak, and habitually do, determines the outcomes (also known as R.A.M.= Results, Achievements, Manifestations) in our lives, good, bad, or ugly. We will cover this in more detail in the *secret* of Paradigms/Mindsets (the development and effects)

*Finally, brothers, whatever is true, whatever is honorable, whatever is just, whatever is pure, whatever is lovely, whatever is commendable, if there is any excellence, if there is anything worthy of praise, **think about these things**.*

~Philippians 4:8, emphasis mine

-What are the eight things that we are too let our minds dwell on? (Philippians 4:8)

TRUE: alēthēs (*al-ay-thace'*)=From G1 (as a negative particle) and G2990; *true* (as *not concealing*): - true, truly, truth. **G2990: lanthanō (*lan-than'-o*)**=A prolonged form of a primary verb, which is used only as an alternate in certain tenses; to *lie hid* (literally or figuratively); often used adverbially *unwittingly:* - be hid, be ignorant of, unawares.

HONORABLE/HONEST: Semnos (*sem-nos'*)=From G4576; *venerable*, that is, *honorable:* - grave, honest. G4576: sebomai (*seb'-om-ahee*)=Middle voice of an apparently primary verb; to *revere*, that is, *adore:* - devout, religious, worship.

JUST: dikaios (*dik'-ah-yos*)=From G1349; *equitable* (in character or act); by implication *innocent, holy* (absolutely or relatively): - just, meet, right (-eous). **G3149: dikē (*dee'-kay*)**=Probably from G1166; *right* (as self-*evident*), that is, *justice* (the principle, a decision, or its execution): - judgment, punish, vengeance. **G1166: deiknuō (*dike-noo'-o*)**=A prolonged form of an obsolete primary of the same meaning; to *show* (literally or figuratively): - shew.

PURE: hagnos (*hag-nos'*)=From the same as G40; properly *clean*, that is, (figuratively) *innocent, modest, perfect:* - chaste, clean, pure. **G40: hagios (*hag'-ee-os*)**=From ἅγος hagos (an *awful* thing) *sacred* (physically *pure*, morally *blameless* or *religious*, ceremonially *consecrated*): - (most) holy (one, thing), saint.

LOVELY: prosphilēs (*pros-fee-lace'*)=*friendly towards*, that is, *acceptable:* - lovely.

GOOD REPORT: euphēmos (*yoo'-fay-mos)*= *well spoken of,* that is, *reputable:* - of good report.

WORTHY OF VIRTUE/EXCELLENCE: aretē (*ar-et'-ay)*=From the same as G730; properly *manliness* (*valor*), that is, *excellence* (intrinsic or attributed): - praise, virtue. **G730: arrhēn arsēn** *ar'-hrane, ar'-sane* Probably from G142; *male* (as stronger for *lifting*): - male, man. **G142: airō (*ah'ee-ro)*=**A primary verb; to *lift*; by implication to *take up* or *away*; figuratively to *raise* (the voice), *keep in suspense* (the mind); specifically to *sail* away (that is, *weigh anchor*); by Hebraism (compare [H5375]) to *expiate* sin: - away with, bear (up), carry, lift up, loose, make to doubt, put away, remove, take (away, up).

WORTHY OF PRAISE Epainos (*ep'-ahee-nos)*= *laudation;* concretely a *commendable* thing: - praise.

-What are you supposed to do with these eight things? (Philippians 4:8)

LET YOUR MIND DWELL ON THESE THINGS: logizomai (*log-id'-zom-ahee)*= to *take an inventory,* that is, *estimate* (literally or figuratively): - conclude, (ac-) count (of), + despise, esteem, impute, lay, number, reason, reckon, suppose, think (on). **G3056: logos** (*log'-os*+=From G3004; something *said* (including the *thought*); by implication a *topic* (subject of discourse), also *reasoning* (the mental faculty) or *motive*; by extension a *computation*; specifically (with the article in John) the Divine *Expression* (that is, *Christ*): - account, cause, communication, X concerning, doctrine, fame, X have to do, intent, matter, mouth, preaching, question, reason, + reckon, remove, say (-ing), shew, X speaker, speech, talk, thing, + none of these things move me, tidings, treatise, utterance, word, work. **G3004: legō (*leg'-o*=**A primary verb; properly to "lay" forth, that is, (figuratively) *relate* (in words [usually of systematic or set *discourse*; whereas G2036 and G5346 generally refer to an *individual* expression or speech respectively; while G4483 is properly to *break silence* merely, and G2980 means an *extended* or random harangue]); by implication to *mean:* - ask, bid, boast, call, describe, give out, name, put forth, say (-ing, on), shew, speak, tell, utter.

NOTE: These words are to be thought about (dwelling on) like a verb and not "a passing thought" (a noun) *instead of* letting/allowing your mind to dwell on whatever is a lie, dishonest, wrong, impure, ugly, bad report, mediocrity, grumbling and complaining, criticizing.

> *Do not be conformed to this world, but be transformed by the renewal of your mind, that by testing you may discern what is the will of God, what is good and acceptable and perfect.*
> ~Romans 12:2

-What should we **NOT BE** *to this world?* (Romans 12:2)

CONFORMED: suschēmatizō (*soos-khay-mat-id'-zo)*= to *fashion alike*, that is, *conform* to the same pattern (figuratively): - conform to, fashion self, according to. Like fitting into a Jello mold.

-What should we **BE** *in this world?* (Romans 12:2)

TRANSFORMED: metamorphoō (*met-am-or-fo'-o)*= to *transform* (literally or figuratively "metamorphose"): - change, transfigure, transform. Like a butterfly being set free from a cocoon.

THE WORLD DEFINED

> *Do not love the world, nor the things in the world. If anyone loves the world, the love of the Father is not in him. For all that is in the world, the lust of the flesh and the lust of the eyes and the boastful pride of life is* **NOT** *from the Father but is from the world. And the world is passing away, and also its lusts; but the one who does the will of God abides forever.*
> ~I John 2:15–17, emphasis mine

NOTE: When the Word in John 3:16 says, "For God so loved the world (the people of the world, not the world system)...eternal life is hinged on the people of the world believing (trusting in, clinging to, relying on, adhering to, cleaving to) Jesus.

> *And even if our gospel (Good News about the Death, Burial, Resurrection) is veiled (hidden) to those who are perishing (those who have not believed in Jesus), in whose case **the god of this world (the d-evil)** has blinded the minds of the unbelieving, that they might not see the light of the gospel of the glory of Christ, who is the image of God."*
> ~2 Corinthians 4:3–4, 1 Corinthians 15:1, John 1:1, 14
> emphasis and additions mine

-Who is the "god of this world"? (2 Corinthians 4:3-4)

-What does the "god of this world" do to the minds? (2 Corinthians 4:3-4)

-What are the eyes blinded from seeing? (2 Corinthians 4:3-4)

> *"Set your minds on things that are above, not on things that are on earth (the world).*
> ~Colossians 3:2, addition mine

-What **ARE** we to set our mind on? (Colossians 3:2)

-What are our minds **NOT** to be set on? (Colossians 3:2)

> *For those who live according to the flesh set their minds on the things of the flesh, but those who live according to the Spirit set their minds on the things of the Spirit. For to set the mind on the flesh is death, but to set the mind on the Spirit is life and peace."*
> ~Romans 8:5–6

-What should we NOT set our minds on? (Romans 8:5-6)

-What ARE we to set our minds on? (Romans 8:5–6)

-What is the mind set on the flesh? (Romans 8:5–6)

-What is the mind set on the Spirit? (Romans 8:5–6)

> *We destroy arguments and every lofty opinion raised against the knowledge of God, and take every thought/imagination captive to obey Christ.*
> ~2 Corinthians 10:5, addition mine

-What are we destroying when we take every thought/imagination? (2 Corinthians 10:5)

-Why do we take every thought/imagination? (2 Corinthians 10:5)

SPEAK: "...out of the abundance (overflow) of the heart/mind the *mouth speaks*." (Luke 6:45)

-What does the mouth speak? (Luke 6:45)

I believe that *speaking* is the *reflection of the mind, the thinking, the thought process.* Just because we have a thought does not mean that we have to express that thought. We have the power to freely choose to be quiet. The mouth is the great revealer of the mind/heart.

> **IF** *you have been foolish in exalting yourself* **OR** *if you have plotted evil,* **PUT YOUR HAND ON YOUR MOUTH.** *For the churning of milk produces butter, and the pressing of the nose brings forth blood; so the churning of anger* **PRODUCES** *strife?*
> ~Pro-Verbs 30:32–33, emphasis mine

-*What action should you do if you have been foolish in exalting yourself or plotting evil?*
> ~Pro-Verbs 30:32

-What two actions are related to the churning of anger? (Pro-Verbs 30:33)

-What is the cause and effect of agitating (speaking anger) (Pro-Verbs 30:33)

NOTE: It is what is put in the churn (your heart and your mind) combined with the agitator (your mouth and tongue) that produces something. If you churn anger, you produce strife, if your churn/heart/mind is filled with love you produce, in the words of the Elvis song, *"a hunka a hunk of churning love."*

> *Whoever guards his mouth preserves his life; he who opens wide his lips comes to ruin."*
> ~Pro-Verbs 13:3

-What do you preserve when you guard your mouth? (Pro-Verbs 13:3)

-What do you come to when you open wide your lips? (Pro-Verbs 13:3)

> *Let no corrupting talk come out of your mouths, but only such as is good for building up, as fits the occasion, that it may give grace to those who hear.*
> ~Ephesians 4:29

-What should you **NOT** allow to come out of your mouth (which is a reflection of what you are thinking? (Ephesians 4:29)

-What **SHOULD** you allow to come out of your mouth? (Ephesians 4:29)

-What do you give when you don't allow corrupt talk to come out of your mouth, but instead only allow good to come out? (Ephesians 4:29)

Know this, my beloved brothers: let every person be quick to hear, slow to speak, slow to anger;

~James 1:19

-What should you be quick to and slow to do? (James 1:19)

Let your speech always be gracious, seasoned with salt, so that you may know how you ought to answer each person.

~Colossians 4:6

Why should your speech always be gracious and seasoned with salt? (Colossians 4:6)

Let there be no filthiness nor foolish talk nor crude joking, which are out of place, but instead let there be thanksgiving.

~Ephesians 5:4

-What should you **NOT** allow? (Ephesians 5:4)

  a.

  b.

  c.

-What is filthiness, foolish talk, and crude talking considered to be? (Ephesians 5:4)

-Instead of filthiness, foolish talk, or crude joking, what should there be? (Ephesians 5:4)

A soft answer turns away wrath, but a harsh word stirs up anger."

~Pro-Verbs 15:1

-What turns away wrath? (Pro-Verbs 15:1)

-What stirs up anger? (Pro-verbs 15:1)

For by your words you will be justified, and by your words you will be condemned.

~Matthew 12:37

-By what two things will your words do? (Matthew 12:37)
1.
2.

Set a guard, O Lord, over my mouth; keep watch over the door of my lips!

~Psalm 141:3

-What should we set over our mouth? (Psalm 141:3)

-What should we keep over the door of our lips? (Psalm 141:3)

If anyone thinks he is religious and does not bridle his tongue but deceives his heart, this person's religion is worthless.

~James 1:26

-What will deceive your heart/mind? (James 1:26)

-What will your religion be considered? (James 1:26)

A fool gives full vent to his spirit, but a wise man quietly holds it back.

~Pro-Verbs 29:11

-What is someone who gives full vent to his spirit? (Pro-Verbs 29:11)

-What does a quiet man do? (Pro-Verbs 29:11)

The heart of the righteous ponders how to answer, but the mouth of the wicked pours out evil things.

~Pro-Verbs 15:28

-What does a righteous man ponder?

-What does the mouth of the wicked do?

> *Even a fool who keeps silent is considered wise; when he closes his lips, he is deemed intelligent.*
>
> ~Pro-Verbs 17:28

-What is a fool who keeps silent considered to be?

-What makes a fool seem intelligent?

> *A gentle tongue is a tree of life, but perverseness in it breaks the spirit.*
>
> ~Pro-Verbs 15:4

-What is a gentle tongue considered to be?

-What does perverseness (of tongue) do to the spirit?

> *But no human being can tame the tongue. It is a restless evil, full of deadly poison. With it we bless our Lord and Father, and with it we curse people who are made in the likeness of God. From the same mouth come blessing and cursing. My brothers, these things ought not to be so.*
>
> ~James 3:8–10

-Can any human tame the tongue? (James 3:8–10)

-What is the tongue considered to be and full of? (James 3:8–10)

-What do we do with the untamed tongue that is a restless evil, full of deadly poison? (James 3:8–10)

-Who do we curse with the untamed tongue, that is full of restless evil, and full of deadly poison? (James 3:8–10)

To speak evil of no one, to avoid quarreling, to be gentle, and to show perfect courtesy toward all people."

~Titus 3:2

-Who are we to speak evil of? (Titus 3:2)

-What are we to avoid? (Titus 3:2)

-What are we to be and to show? (Titus 3:2)

I tell you, on the day of judgment people will give account for every careless word they speak.

~Matthew 12:36

-What will people give on the day of judgement?

A word fitly spoken is like apples of gold in a setting of silver.

~Pro-Verbs 25:11

-What is a word fitly spoken like? (Pro-Verbs 25:11)

Do not repay evil for evil or reviling for reviling, but on the contrary, bless, for to this you were called, that you may obtain a blessing."

~1Peter 3:9

-What are we **NOT** to repay? (1 Peter 3:9)

-What are we **TO** repay when given evil or reviling? (1 Peter 3:9)

-What is this considered to be? (1 Peter 3:9)

-What will we obtain as we walk in this calling? (1 Peter 3:9)

For whoever desires to love life and see good days, let him keep

his tongue from evil and his lips from speaking deceit.
~1 Peter 3:10

-What will ensure that you love life and see good days? (1 Peter 3:10)

Therefore, having put away falsehood, let each one of you speak the truth with his neighbor, for we are members one of another.
~Ephesians 4:25

-What must we put away and then do?

-What are we members of?

Whoever restrains his words has knowledge, and he who has a cool spirit is a man of understanding.
~Pro-Verbs 17:27

-What do you have when you restrain your words? (Pro-Verbs 17:27)

-What is someone who has a cool spirit? (Pro-Verbs 17:27)

So also the tongue is a small member, yet it boasts of great things. How great a forest is set ablaze by such a small fire!"
~James 3:35

-What size tongue do you have as a member of your body? (James 3:35)

-What can that small member of your body do? (James 3:5)

For we all stumble in many ways. And if anyone does not stumble in what he says, he is a perfect man, able also to bridle his whole body.
~James 3:2

-What do we all do? (James 3:2)

-What are you if you don't stumble? (James 3:2)

> *Better is a poor person who walks in his integrity than one who is crooked in speech and is a fool.*
>
> ~Pro-Verbs 19:1

-What are you if you walk in integrity? (Pro-Verbs 19:1)

- If you don't walk in integrity, what are you? (Pro-Verbs 19:1)

> *She opens her mouth with wisdom, and the teaching of kindness is on her tongue.*
>
> ~Pro-Verbs 31:26

-What is on the tongue of one who opens her mouth with wisdom? (Pro-Verbs 31:26)

> *Even in your thoughts, do not curse the king, nor in your bedroom curse the rich, for a bird of the air will carry your voice, or some winged creature tell the matter.*
>
> ~Ecclesiastes 10:20

-What is the cause and effect when you curse the king or the rich? (Ecclesiastes 10:20)

> *A lying tongue hates its victims, and a flattering mouth works ruin.*
>
> ~Pro-Verbs 26:28

-Who does a lying tongue hate? (Pro-Verbs 26:28)

-What does a flattering mouth work? (Pro-Verbs 26:28)

> *There are six things that the Lord hates, seven that are an abomination to him: haughty eyes, a lying tongue, and hands that shed*

innocent blood, a heart that devises wicked plans, feet that make haste to run to evil, a false witness who breathes out lies, and one who sows discord among brothers.

~Pro-Verbs 6:16–19)

-What are the six things that the Lord hates/seven that are an abomination to him?(Pro-Verbs 6:16-19)

1.
2.
3.
4.
5.
6.
7.

-What do you think that you should hate, especially in your own life?

Death and life are in the power of the tongue, and those who love it will eat its fruits.

~Pro-Verbs 18:21

-What two things are in the power of the tongue? (Pro-Verbs 18:21)

1.
2.

A fool's lips walk into a fight, and his mouth invites a beating.
~Pro-Verbs 18:6

-What does a fools lips walk into and what does his mouth invite? (Pro-Verbs 18:6)

A time to tear, and a time to sew; a time to keep silence, and a time to speak.

~Ecclesiastes 3:7

-What is there a time to do?
1.
2.
3.
4.

> *Let all bitterness and wrath and anger and clamor and slander*
> *be put away from you, along with all malice.*
>   ~Ephesians 4:31

-What should be put away from you? (Ephesians 4:31)
1.
2.
3.
4.
5.
6.

BITTERNESS: Pikria (*pik-ree'-ah)*=From G4089; *acridity* (especially *poison*), literally or figuratively: - bitterness. **G4089: pikros (*pik-ros')=** (through the idea of *piercing*); *sharp* (*pungent*), that is, *acrid* (literally or figuratively): - bitter

WRATH: thumos (*thoo-mos')=From G2380; *passion* (as if *breathing* hard): - fierceness, indignation, wrath G2380:** thuō (*thoo'-o)=*A primary verb; properly to *rush* (*breathe* hard, *blow*, *smoke*), that is, (by implication) to *sacrifice* (properly by fire, but generally); by extension to *immolate* (*slaughter* for any purpose): - kill, (do) sacrifice, slay.

ANGER: orgē (*or-gay')* =From G3713; properly *desire* (as a *reaching* forth or *excitement* of the mind), that is, (by analogy) violent *passion* (*ire*, or [justifiable] *abhorrence*); by implication *punishment:* - anger, indignation, vengeance, wrath. =Middle voice of apparently a prolonged form of an obsolete primary); to *stretch* oneself, that is, *reach* out after (*long* for): - covet after, desire.

CLAMOR: kraugē (*krow-gay'*)=From G2896; an *outcry* (in notification, tumult or grief): - clamour, cry (-ing). **G2896: krazō (*krad'-zo*)**=A primary verb; properly to "croak" (as a raven) or *scream*, that is, (generally) to *call* aloud (*shriek, exclaim, intreat*): - cry (out).

SLANDER: blasphēmia (*blas-fay-me'-ah*)=From G989; *vilification* (especially against God): - blasphemy, evil speaking, railing. **G989: blasphēmos (*blas'-fay-mos*)**= *scurrilous*, that is, *calumnious* (against man), or (specifically) *impious* (against God): - blasphemer (-mous), railing.

MALICE: kakia (*kak-ee'-ah*)=From G2556; *badness*, that is, (subjectively) *depravity*, or (actively) *malignity*, or (passively) *trouble:* - evil, malice (-iousness), naughtiness, wickedness.

G2556: kakos (*kak-os'*)=Apparently a primary word; *worthless* (*intrinsically* such; whereas G4190 properly refers to *effects*), that is, (subjectively) *depraved*, or (objectively) *injurious:* - bad, evil, harm, ill, noisome, wicked.

-Instead of bitterness, wrath, anger, clamor, slander, and malice, what should we be in the way that we think, speak and act? (Ephesians 4:32)

-Who has forgiven you? (Ephesians 4:32)

> *The thoughts of the wicked are an abomination to the Lord, but gracious words are pure.*
>
> ~Pro-Verbs 15:26

-What are the thoughts of the wicked? (Pro-Verbs 15:26)

-What are words of the pure? (Pro-Verbs 15:26)

> *The tongue of the wise commends knowledge, but the mouths of fools pour out folly.*
>
> ~Pro-Verbs 15:2

-What does the tongue of the wise commend? (Pro-Verbs 15:2)

-What does the mouth of the fool pour out? (Pro-Verbs 15:2)

> *The mouth of the righteous brings forth wisdom, but the perverse tongue will be cut off.*
> ~Pro-Verbs 10:31

-What does the righteous bring forth? (Pro-verbs 10:31)

-What will happen to the perverse tongue? (Pro-Verbs 10:31)

NOTE: Do you get the idea that God cares what we are thinking about and what we say and do?

DO/ACTION: "Faith without *works* is dead." (James 2:17, emphasis mine)

> *Faith without corresponding actions is of none effect.*
> ~James 2:17 the Weymouth translation.

> *Faith (what you believe that is the substance of things (tangibles, what you want) confidently expected/hoped for, the evidence/the hard cold facts of things (tangibles, what you want)* **NOT SEEN** *(since we walk by faith and not by our senses of sight, sound, smell, taste, touch).*
> ~James 2:17, Hebrews 11:1 with emphasis, additions, and commentary mine, Ruminator Style

I believe that you can *think* about something and *talk* about it all day long but if you don't *do* something about what you are *thinking and speaking*, all that you have are thoughts and words with *no results*. There are two aspects about doing or not doing. You can't do anything to get spiritually right with God, but if you don't put your faith in to corresponding actions your faith will be of none effect or dead.

For by grace you have been saved through faith. And this is not your own doing; it is the gift of God, not a result of works, so that no one may boast. For we are his workmanship, created in Christ Jesus for good works, which God prepared beforehand, that we should walk in them."

~Ephesians 2:8–10

-How have you been saved? (Ephesians 2:8)

-Is salvation of your own doing? (Ephesians 2:8)

-If it is not of yourself, what is it? (Ephesians 2:8)

-Is salvation a result of your works? (Ephesians 2:9)

-What is your salvation not of your works? (Ephesians 2:9)

-What are we? (Ephesians 2:10)

-What were we created in Christ Jesus for (2 Corinthians 2:17, 21) (Ephesians 2:10)

-When did God prepare these things for us to do? (Ephesians 2:10)

-What should we do the things in? (Ephesians 2:10)

What good is it, my brothers, if someone says he has faith but does not have works? Can that faith save him? If a brother or sister is poorly clothed and lacking in daily food, and one of you says to them, "Go in peace, be warmed and filled," without giving them the things needed for the body, what good is that? So also, faith by itself if it does not have works, is dead. But someone will say, "You have faith and I have works." Show me your faith apart from your works, and I will show you my faith by my works.

~James 2:14–20

-Is it any good for you to say that you have faith but does not have works? (James 2:14)

-Can that type of faith save you? (James 1:14)

-What is faith without works? (James 1:17)

-What example is given of faithless works? (James 1:15-16)

-By what should we show? (James 1:18)

> And let our people learn to **devote themselves to good works**, so as to help cases of urgent need, and not be unfruitful."
> ~Titus 3:14

-What should we learn to do? (Titus 3:14)

> Do you want to be shown, you foolish person, that faith apart from works is useless? Was not Abraham our father justified by works when he offered up his son Isaac on the altar? You see that faith was active along with his works, and faith was completed by his works; and the Scripture was fulfilled that says, "Abraham believed God, and it was counted to him as righteousness"—and he was called a friend of God. You see that a person is justified by works and not by faith alone.
> ~James 2:20–24

-What is faith apart from works? (James 2:20)

-How was Abraham justified? (James 2:21)

-What was Abraham's faith working with? (James 2:21)

-What was the cause and effect of Abraham's faith working with his works?

-What did Abraham do? (James 2:23)

-What was Abraham's belief reckoned to him as? (James 2:23, Genesis 15:6)

-What was Abraham called as a result of his faith? (James 2:23, 2 Chronicles 20:7, Isaiah 41:8)

> *The saying is trustworthy, and I want you to insist on these things, so that those who have believed in God may be careful to devote themselves to good works. These things are excellent and profitable for people.*
> ~Titus 3:8

-What should those who are have believed in God be careful to do? (Titus 3:8)

-What two things are these for people?
1.
2.

> *In the same way, let your light shine before others, so that they may see your good works and give glory to your Father who is in heaven.*
> ~Matthew 5:16

-What are we supposed to do/let/allow? (Matthew 5:16)

-What is the same way that we are to let/allow our light to shine before others? (Matthew 5:14–15)

> *For God is not unjust so as to overlook your work and the love that you have shown for his name in serving the saints, as you still do.*
> ~Hebrews 6:10

-Does God overlook your work and your live that you have shown for his name? (Hebrews 6:10)

-Where is our work and love directed to in serving? (Hebrews 6:10)

Equip you with everything good that you may do his will, working in us that which is pleasing in his sight, through Jesus Christ, to whom be glory forever and ever. Amen.

~Hebrews 13:21

-What does he equip us with and why? (Hebrews 13:21)

-What are these works in His sight? (Hebrews 13:21)

-What pleases God? (Hebrews 11:6)

-Who are these works through? (Hebrews 13:21)

-How long will this glory be? (Hebrews 13:21)

But be doers of the word, and not hearers only, deceiving yourselves. For if anyone is a hearer of the word and not a doer, he is like a man who looks intently at his natural face in a mirror. For he looks at himself and goes away and at once forgets what he was like. But the one who looks into the perfect law, the law of liberty, and perseveres, being no hearer who forgets but a doer who acts, he will be blessed in his doing. If anyone thinks he is religious and does not bridle his tongue but deceives his heart, this person's religion is worthless.

~James 1:22–27

You are my friends if you do what I command you.

~John 15:14

-What is the true sign of your friendship with God? (John 15:14)

But the one who looks into the perfect law, the law of liberty, and perseveres, being not a hearer who forgets but a doer who acts, he will be blessed in his doing.

~James 1:25

-What must you do with the perfect law, the law of liberty (in the Word of God)? (James 1:25)

-What must you do? (James 1:25)

-In your perseverance (not giving up) what should you NOT be? (James 1:25)

-What does someone who is only a hearer do? (James 1:25)

-Instead of just being a hearer who forgets what the perfect law, the law of liberty says, what should we be? (James 1:25)

-When you not only hear but do the Word, what are you? (James 1:25)

> *For it is not the hearers of the law who are righteous before God, but the doers of the law who will be justified.*
> ~Romans 2:13

-Who are righteous before God that will be justified? (Romans 2:13)

Well, that was a long section but I believe that as you renew your mind with the Word of God and follow Joshua 1:8, that you will experience prosperity (enough to meet your needs and an overflow to help others) and good (not bad) success as you accomplish the purposes of God in your spiritual life, your personal life, your relationships with others, and your business life.

DO NOT BE WEAK AND DISCOURAGED

*Only be **strong** and very **courageous**; be careful to do according to all the law which Moses My servant commanded you; do not turn from it to the right or to the left, so that you may have success wherever you go.*

~Joshua 1:7

STRONG: châzaq (*khaw-zak'*)=A primitive root; to *fasten* upon; hence to *seize, be strong* (figuratively *courageous*, causatively *strengthen, cure, help, repair, fortify*), *obstinate*; to *bind, restrain, conquer*: - aid, amend, X calker, catch, cleave, confirm, be constant, constrain, continue, be of good (take) courage (-ous, -ly), encourage (self), be established, fasten, force, fortify, make hard, harden, help, (lay) hold (fast), lean, maintain, play the man, mend, become (wax) mighty, prevail, be recovered, repair, retain, seize, be (wax) sore, strengthen(self), be stout, be (make, shew, wax) strong (-er), be sure, take (hold), be urgent, behave self valiantly, withstand.

COURAGEOUS: 'âmats (*aw-mats'*)=A primitive root; to *be alert*, physically (on foot) or mentally (in courage): - confirm, be courageous (of good courage, stedfastly minded, strong, stronger), establish, fortify, harden, increase, prevail, strengthen (self), make strong (obstinate, speed).

The phrase, "be strong and courageous" occurs eight times in Deuteronomy and Joshua in reference to crossing into the Promised Land. In Joshua 1:7, the word "very" is added to courageous.

1. Deuteronomy 31:6
2. Deuteronomy 31:7
3. Deuteronomy 31:23
4. Joshua 1:6
5. Joshua 1:7
6. Joshua 1:9
7. Joshua 1:18
8. Joshua 10:25

VERY: me'ôd (*meh-ode'*)=From the same as H181; properly *vehemence*, that is, (with or without preposition) *vehemently*; by implication *wholly, speedily*, etc. (often with other words as an intensive or superlative; especially when repeated): - diligently, especially, exceeding (-ly), far, fast, good, great (-ly), X louder and louder, might (-ily, -y), (so) much, quickly, (so) sore, utterly, very (+ much, sore), well. **H181: 'ûd** (*ood*) =From an unused root meaning to *rake* together; a *poker* (for *turning* or *gathering* embers): - (fire-) brand.

The children of Israel were about to cross over into the promised land that God had given them, but they were warned to be strong and courageous. Why? Because they would have every opportunity to be weak and discouraged. The same advice goes for us today on our quest for success. There are multiple promises found in the Bible (aka The Manufacturer's Handbook) but we still have to be careful to be strong and courageous. I believe that the Bible is also the ultimate book for success. The Bible aka The Word of God, The Manufacturer's Hand, The Communication with God Codebook, and as we said, The Biblical Book of Prosperity and Success filled with Laws, Principles, and Codes to live life to the fullest. In the next secret to success (#13) we will go more into depth on strength and courage in relation to thinking, speaking, and acting by faith and not by sight.

Then Joshua commanded the officers of the people saying, pass through the midst of the camp and command the people, saying prepare provisions for yourselves, for within three days you are to cross this Jordan (River) to go in to possess the land which the Lord your God is giving you to possess.

~Joshua 1:1–11

It was not that they would possibly be given a Promised Land, it was a fact, it was promised, and they would possess it, but they had to do the possessing part. The same is true with what you have been promised in Joshua 1:8, to be prosperous and to have success. We must do like the children of promise, before our prosperity and success comes, we must "prepare provisions" before the crossing of "the Rubicon." A Rubicon means "passing a point of no return," that refers to the crossing of the river Rubicon by Julius Caesar in early January 49 B.C. Their Rubicon was the Jordan River. Our Rubicon may be doubt, unbelief, fear, logic. We must keep our eyes on what lies beyond the Rubicon/Jordan River. On the other side of the Jordan River was a land that flowed with milk and honey among other wonderful things. Again, in our next secret, we will see The Grasshopper Principle.

Then Joshua said to the people, consecrate yourselves (today is implied) for tomorrow the Lord will do wonders among you."

~Joshua 3:5, addition mine

In Joshua 1:10–11, they were instructed to prepare provisions. In three days they would be crossing over for the purpose of possessing the Promised Land. Their provisions most likely were food, water, weapons, etc. Our provisions may be going to school, getting an internship in the desired profession, saving money, etc. **NOW**, two days had passed and "tomorrow" they would be crossing over, with their prepared provisions, cross over and see the wonders of possessing the land in the face of giants. For you, you could be starting your own business, stepping out in faith, becoming prosperous and successful, because you know the secret and you will see the wonders of God in the Promised Land.

THE GRASSHOPPER PRINCIPLE

There also we saw the Nephilim (the sons of Anak are part of the Nephilim); and **we became like grasshoppers in our own sight, and so we were in their sight.**
~Numbers 13:33, addition and emphasis mine

In the #12 secret to success we mentioned the secret of *being strong and courageous.* In #13 we see the *reconnaissance mission* as twelve of the elite men from the tribes of Israel were sent into the Promised Land to scope out the territory. There were twelve reports, ten bad reports and two good reports.

Reports are like the phrase **GODISNOWHERE**. Some reports will see (1) God is **NO** where and some will see (2) God is **NOW** here. It all depends on *how you look at the circumstances and situations* that will determine your outcome.

God spoke to Moses again and told him to send out twelve *for the purpose of spying out the land of Canaan.* This was not just *some land* but the land, *"which I am going to give to the sons of Israel."* The twelve men were not just average guys, but they were the heads of the tribes, they were the elite, they were the Navy Seals of the day. (Numbers 13:1—15) Moses called Hoshea, the son of Nun, Joshua.

NOTE: No, Joshua the son of Nun does not mean that his mama was a nun in a convent, and it does not mean that he had no parents, Joshua the son of None.

The name Joshua means "salvation." Jesus' name in the Hebrew

Yeshua (God is salvation) the Messiah, the Christ, the Anointed One. When Moses was telling them about the Promised Land, the people wanted to spy out the land and it seemed good to Moses. (Deuteronomy 1:22)

Back in the day, names had meanings. For example Jesus (God is salvation) Immanuel (God with us) The Christ (Messiah, the Anointed One).

NOTE: In life and business it is good for us to collect as much information as we can about everything from what we are trying to sell or do and as much as we can about our competition and potential troubles that may arise. Cover your bases.

NOTE TO THE NOTE: God allowed them to go spy out the land (a reconnaissance mission (investigation, scouting, inspection) , because they wanted to, but it was not to see the problems but to verify to them that the promise was true.

NOTE TO THE NOTE TO THE NOTE: It is a good thing to scope out your competition, the financial landscape, the market for your services.

RECONNAISSANCE ORDERS (Numbers 13:17–20)

1. Go into the Negev (a large desert region in southern Israel)
2. Then go up into the hill country
3. See what the land is like
4. See it the people who live in it are strong or weak
5. See if there are few or many people
6. See how is the land in which they live
7. Is the land good or bad
8. See how the cities are where they live
9. Are the cities open camps or with fortifications
10. See how the land is
11. Is the land fat or lean
12. Are there trees in the land or not

13. Make an effort to get some of the fruit of the land (the time was the time of the first ripe grapes) They cut down a branch with a single cluster of grapes that had to be carried by two men with some pomegranates and figs.

The spies went and returned after *40 days* of reconnaissance.

NOTE: Success is not *instant success* but there is a time factor. Many people spin their wheels for years and never get anywhere with their desires, dreams, visions, imaginations, inspirations, thoughts, ideas, goals, and plans. Here is a formula for accomplishing your purposes.

DESIRES, DREAMS, VISIONS, IMAGINATIONS, INSPIRATIONS, THOUGHTS, IDEAS, GOALS, PLANS

-

LOGIC

+

FAITH/BELIEF

+

SPEAKING/CONFESSION

+

ACTIONS

+

PERSEVERENCE

=

R.A.M.

=

RESULTS, ACHEIVEMENTS, MANIFESTAIONS

THE REPORTS

When they returned back (from the reconnaissance mission) from spying out the land, at the end of forty days, they reported back to Moses and Aaron and to all the congregation of the sons of Israel. They brought back word to them and to all the congregation and showed them the fruit of the land (Numbers 13:25–26)

Thus they told him, and said, we went into the land where you sent us (remember in Deuteronomy 1:22 they wanted to spy out the land), and it certainly does flow with milk and honey, and this fruit.
~Numbers 13:27, addition mine

NOTE: So far, so good. The report is positive and affirms what God had told them.

Now, there was a negative shift in the report. Remember Pro-Verb 23:7, "As a man (or spies) thinketh in their hearts/minds so they **ARE**." Remember that out of abundance (overflow) of the heart/mind the mouth speaks." (Luke 6:45) The ten spies minds and hearts are revealed by the next word in Numbers 13:28, "**NEVERTHELESS**"

NEVERTHELESS: 'ephes *(eh'-fes)*=From H656; *cessation*, that is, an *end* (especially of the earth); often used adverbially *no further*; also (like H6466) the *ankle* (in the dual), as being the extremity of the leg or foot: - ankle, but (only), end, howbeit, less than nothing, nevertheless (where), no, none (beside), not (any, -withstanding), thing of nought, save (-ing), there, uttermost part, want, without (cause). **H656:** 'âphês *(aw-face')*=A primitive root; to *disappear*, that is, *cease:* - be clean gone (at an end, brought to nought), fail.

NOTE: Many people have desires, goals, dreams, visions, imaginations, inspirations, thoughts, ideas, goals, and plans, but when they are faced with obstructions, obstacles, mountains, giants they **GIVE UP.** The have a **NEVERTHELESS MENTALITY.** A nevertheless mentality plus a grasshopper mentality turns into a failure and poverty mentality.

NEVERTHELESS, *the people who live in the land are strong, and the cities are fortified and very large; and* **MOREOVER**; *we saw the descendants of Anak there.*
~Numbers 13:28, emphasis mine

NOTE: When you combine a **NEVERTHELESS MENTALITY**

and a **MOREOVER MENTALITY** with a **GRASSHOPPER MENTALITY** you have a **FAILURE MENTALITY**.

THE BAD REPORT FROM A NEVERTHELESS, MOREOVER, GRASSHOPPER, FAILURE MENTALITY (Numbers 13:28–29)

1. The people who live in the land are strong
2. The cities are fortified
3. The cities are very large (indicating a large amount of people living in the cities
4. We saw the descendants of Anak there
5. Amalek is living in the land
6. The Hittites are living in the land
7. The Jebusites are living in the land
8. The Amorites are living in the hill country
9. The Canaanites are living by the sea and by the side of the Jordan

NOTE: Everything that the ten spies reported back was *true*. Their report was very *factual*. There is a difference between *facts/reality* and **TRUTH**. Remember **TRUTH** trumps reality. Jesus defined truth as the Father's Word, "Sanctify them by **TRUTH**, Thy Word is **TRUTH**." (John 17:17)

> "We don't deny reality because reality is real. We don't deny reality, but we don't allow reality the right to rule our lives, emotions, outcomes, and destiny."
> ~Rodfucious, from *The Quirky Wit and Wisdom of Rofucious*

NOTE TO THE NOTE: When people are negative, negativity infiltrates and spread to those who are listening. This is what happened during this negative report.

Then Caleb quieted the people before Moses and said…"
~Numbers 13:30

THE GOOD REPORT (Numbers 13:30)

After Caleb quieted the people who were stirred up by the negativity of the bad report.

> "...*We should by* **ALL MEANS** *(by everything that we've got) go up and take possession it (the Promised Land) that the ten spies said not to possess)* **FOR WE SHALL SURELY OVERCOME."**
> ~Numbers 13:30, emphasis and addition mine

NOTE: Caleb was speaking words of faith about a future victory. Caleb was practicing what Abraham did by, "calling things that are **NOT** as though they **WERE"** (Romans 4:17) instead of doing what the ten negative spies did and "called things that **ARE** as if they will **NEVER CHANGE."** (Rodfucious)

The negative spies countered with more negativity.

> *But the men who had gone up with him said, we are* **NOT ABLE** *to go up against the people, for* **THEY ARE TOO STRONG FOR US**.
> ~Numbers 13:31, emphasis mine

Then they began to underscore why they can't go in and possess the land that God had already given them. They began to speak what they saw with their senses. They were leaning on and trusting their **LOWER FACTULTIES** and not factoring in the **HIGHER FACULTIES.**

The **LOWER FACULTIES** are what we have in common with animals, like dogs, snakes, pigs, etc. The ten spies with the negative report were only using the **LOWER FACULTIES.** What separates us from the animals is the **HIGHER FACULTIES.** They ten spies who gave out a negative report were walking in fear and not faith.

THE LOWER FACULTIES

1. Sight
2. Sound
3. Smell
4. Taste
5. Touch

THE HIGHER FACULTIES

1. Perception
2. Imagination
3. Will
4. Reason
5. Intuition
6. Memory

It is with the **HIGHER FACULTIES OF THE MIND** that we can shift and change our **PARADIGMS/MINDSETS** from a negative/bad report into a positive mindset/a positive report.

So they gave out to the sons of Israel **A BAD REPORT** *of the land which they had spied out, saying, the land through which we have gone, in spying it out is a land that devours its inhabitants; and all the people whom we saw in it are men of great size.*
~Numbers 13:32, emphasis mine

NOTE: A toxic and negative report not only affects the ones giving out the bad report, but it also affects those around them who hear and receive the bad report. The same is true for a good report.

If the Apostle Paul was there, he would counter with,

I CAN DO *all things (including going in and possessing the land that God has promised us) through Christ (the Anointed One and His anointing) who* **STRENGTHENS ME.**
~Philippians 4:13 with additions and emphasis mine, Ruminator Style

GRASSHOPPER THEOLOGY (Numbers 13:33)

There also we saw the Nephilim (the sons of Anak are part of the Nephilim); and we **BECAME** *like grasshoppers* **IN OUR OWN SIGHT**, *and so* **WE WERE IN THEIR SIGHT."**
~Numbers 13:33, emphasis mine

As a man (or a group of spies) thinketh in their hearts/minds **SO THEY ARE**.
~Pro-Verbs 27:3, emphasis and addition mine

...out of the abundance (overflow) of the heart/mind the **MOUTH SPEAKS** *(confesses)*.
~Luke 6:45, emphasis and addition mine

How we think about ourselves and how we speak about ourselves is how we see ourselves and how we see ourselves is how our enemies see us also.

We will discuss this more in the Secrets of Paradigms and Mindsets and how what we think and speak and do will determine the results in our lives.

LEARN THE SECRET

*Not that I speak from want; for I have **learned** to be content in whatever circumstances I am. I know how to get along with humble means, and I also **know** how to live in prosperity; in any and every circumstance **I have learned the secret** of being filled and going hungry, both of having abundance and suffering need.*
                                   ~Philippians 4:11–12, emphasis mine

I like how Paul was on a learning curve. When we stop learning we stop growing. Jesus spoke to a group of people who actually *believed* what He was teaching but told them that there was *another level* of going from *believing* to *knowing*. What took them from merely believing to knowing was;

*"**IF** you abide/continue in My word, **THEN** you are truly disciples of Mine; and you (believers) shall know the truth, and the truth shall make you free.*
                                   ~John 8:31–32, addition and emphasis mine

My friend in the Kingdom faith, Wayne Berry, posted this on Facebook which speaks of this process of learning.

SELF-ADJUSTMENT(s) (Wayne Berry)

Not that I am speaking of being in need, for I have learned in whatever situation I am to be content.
                                                   ~Phil.4:11

The operative word in that verse isn't *content*, it's *learned. Contentment is the goal*, and *learning is the process.* The goal is unreachable without going [through] the process. It's a "strength to strength," "glory to glory" thing. (Ps.84:7 & 2 Cor.3:18)

TO SPEAK OR NOT TO SPEAK FROM WANT, THAT IS THE QUESTION?

Some believe that we are never, ever to express what we want. I disagree. I ask people who are on their journey, "What do you really **WANT**?" I stole that question from Bob Proctor. But didn't Paul tells us, "not that I am speaking from want…" (Philippians 4:11)

WANT: husterēsis (*hoos-ter'-ay-sis*)=From G5302; a *falling short*, that is, (specifically) *penury (extreme poverty, destitution)* : - want.=**G5302: hustereō (*hoos-ter-eh'-o*)**=From G5306; to *be later*, that is, (by implication) to *be inferior*, genitively to *fall short (be deficient)*: - come behind (short), be destitute, fall, lack, suffer need, (be in) want, be the worse. **G5306: husteros (*hoos'-ter-os*=**Comparatively from G5259 (in the sense of *behind*); *later:* - latter.

Philippians 4:11 is **NOT** talking about **NOT** speaking what you want, but do not speak from a position of **WANT.**

> *Not that I am speaking from falling short, penury (extreme poverty, destitution), inferior, deficient, coming from behind, lack, suffering need, to be the worse…"*
> ~Philippians 4:11

That is a big difference from not speaking from wanting something. When Paul wrote this, he was in prison and some people he loved brought him something. Paul used it as an opportunity to teach them on money/finances/wants and needs. (Philippians 4:11–19)

When you combine Philippians 4:11 with Psalm 23:1, you get more insight on this thing called speaking from want.

The Lord is my Shepherd; I shall **NOT WANT**.
                                        ~Psalm 23:1, emphasis mine

WANT: châsêr (*khaw-sare')*=A primitive root; to *lack*; by implication to *fail, want, lessen:* - be abated, bereave, decrease, (cause to) fail, (have) lack, make lower, want.

The Lord is my Shepherd I shall not lack, fail want, lessen, be abated, bereave, decrease, fail, make lower, want.
                                        ~Psalm 23:1, addition mine

So we see that the idea of speaking from want and not wanting does not mean not to want things but realize that you don't have to speak from want, because you have a Shepherd, the God who gives you strength and supply.

I have **STRENGTH** for **ALL THINGS** in Christ (the Anointed One and His anointing)Who empowers me [I am ready for anything and equal to anything through Him Who infuses me with **INNER STRENGTH** into me; I am self-sufficient in Christ's sufficiency].
                ~Philippians 4:13 Amplified Bible with emphasis, additions,
                                        and commentary mine, Ruminator Style

And My God (my Shepherd) will **LIBERALLY SUPPLY** *(fill to the full) your every need/want according to (based on) His riches in glory in Christ Jesus (and their ain't no shortage in glory or the Anointed One and His anointing).*
                ~Philippians 4:19 Amplified Bible with emphasis, additions,
                                        and commentary mine, Ruminator Style

Paul accepted their gifts but told them that;

Not that I seek the gift itself, but I seek for the profit which increase to your account.
                                        ~Philippians 4:17

He goes on to tell them;

but I have received everything in full, and have an **ABUN-DANCE** *; I am* **AMPLY SUPPLIED**…

~Philippians 4:18

No, Paul did not have to speak from **WANT,** because He knew his Shepherd. I'm thinking that IF you are WANTING, then you may need to check out the relationship with the Shepherd.

There are all kinds of books and movies and teachings about how to tap into the "secrets of the universe." They speak of being able to *call on the universe* and attract to them what they speak and want, and the universe delivers like a universal slot machine or a sugar daddy or Santa Claus or a genie just waiting to give you want you want.

I personally believe and have a relationship because of Jesus, *a relationship with the Creator of the universe* who gives me;

every good and perfect gift from above coming down from the Father (the Creator of the universe) of heavenly lights, who does not change like the shifting shadows.

~James 1:17, addition mine

I also have access to the promises of God.

For as many as the promises of God are, **IN HIM** *they are* **YES;** *therefore, through Him also is our* **AMEN** *to the glory of God.*

~2 Corinthians 1:20, emphasis mine

God, the Creator of the universe is also a giver.

Delight yourself (make yourself like clay in the Potters hand) in the Lord (the Potter) and He (God) will give you (plant in you and bring them to pass) the desires (what you want) your heart.

~Psalm 37:4, additions mine

Paul had *learned* **THE SECRET** (before the Secret was a book or movie).

Paul knew some things that he had learned.

KNEW: eidō (*i'-do*)_=A primary verb; used only in certain past tenses, properly to *see* (literally or figuratively); by implication (in the perfect only) to *know*: - be aware, behold, X can (+ not tell), consider, (have) known (-ledge), look (on), perceive, see, be sure, tell, understand, wist, wot.

LEARNED: mueō (*moo-eh'-o*)=From the base of G3466; to *initiate*, that is, (by implication) to *teach:* - instruct G3466: mus-tērion (*moos-tay'-ree-on*)= (to *shut* the mouth); a *secret* or "**mystery**" (through the idea of *silence* imposed by *initiation* into religious rites): - mystery.

Previously we saw that Paul did not speak from want (or lack of provision because he knew the provider) and had learned how to be content in whatever circumstance (good, bad or ugly) that he found himself in. (Philippians 4:11) Now he speaks of the *learned secret* a little more in Philippian 4:12)

- I know how to get along with humble means
- I also know how to live in prosperity

NOTE: Prosperity is not bad and living in humble means does not mean that you are not any less a man or woman of God based on what you've got. Your bank account is *NOT* an indicator of the size of your faith.

- In any and every circumstance I learned the secret.
- The secret of being filled
- The secret of going hungry
- The secret of having abundance
- The secret of suffering need.

The **SECRET** is wrapped up in Philippians 4:13, 19.

I have strength for all thins in Christ Who empowers me [I am ready for anything and equal to anything through Him Who infuses inner strength in me; I am self-sufficient in Christ's sufficiency].
                    ~Philippians 4:13 Amplified Bible

And my God will liberally supply (fill to the full) your every need

according to His riches in glory in Christ Jesus.
~Philippians 4:19 Amplified Bible

When I am faced with circumstances, I like to quote/declare/ confess out lout Philippians 4:19 and put in my specific needs. For example, when I am pumping gas and the prices of gas is $4.25 a gallon, instead of moaning and groaning and blaming the President, I say out loud, "I thank my God that He supplies all of my **GAS NEEDS** (fill in the blank of whatever you need) according to His riches in glory in Christ Jesus and their **AIN'T** no shortage in (1) glory (2) Christ Jesus!

I want to end with this thought. Your prosperity and success is not hinged on how much money or how successful you are. Here is a thought from my last book *Biblical Prosperity And Success Ruminator Style.*

Let's face it, the whole subject of Biblical Prosperity and Success is pretty controversial. While there is nothing inherently wrong with having money or possessions, it is certainly true that the love of money is the root of all kinds of evil. Having great fame and possessions is not always a sign of God's favor just as having few possessions is not necessarily a sign of God's judgement.

The Book of Hebrews includes a chapter often referred to as The Hall of Faith—a list of people who have gone before us who by faith gained the approval and approbation of God. By faith Abel brought God a better offering than Cain, Enoch was taken from this life so that he did not experience death, Noah built an ark to save his family, and others conquered kingdoms, administered justice, shut the mouths of lions, quenched the fury of the flames, escaped the edge of the sword; became powerful in battle and received back their dead, raised to life again. Yet other, equally faithful servants of God were tortured for their faith, faced jeers and flogging, chains and imprisonment, were put to death by stoning, were sawed in two, or killed by the sword. They were destitute, persecuted, and mistreated—the world was not worthy of them.

Biblical success can be defined as accomplishing the purposes of God in our lives. Biblical prosperity can be viewed as having enough to meet our needs and an overflow to help meet the needs of others. In a world of socialism, communism, capitalism, and every other kind of -ism, the question is not what you have, but what are you going to do with it?

Also in *Biblical Prosperity And Success Ruminator Style*, we see the **HALL OF FAITH** (found in Hebrews 11).

While we are talking about the Biblical Principles of Prosperity and Success, I would be remiss in not pointing out that just because someone does not have a lot of prosperity or success in the eyes of the world, it does not make them any less prosperous or successful. I love the Book of Hebrews chapter eleven that is known theologically as "The Hall of Faith." It is a list of people who have come and gone before us (aka the cloud of witnesses in Hebrews 12:1) who by faith gained approval and had wonderful (full of wonder) "pro-vision" (positive revelatory insights into God's prosperity and success). But starting in Hebrews 11:36 there is a shift of thought concerning other saints.

> *And others experienced mocking's and scourging's, yes also chains and imprisonment. They were sawn into, they were tempted, they were put to death with the sword; they went about in sheepskins, in goatskins, being destitute afflicted, ill-treated (men of whom the world was not worthy), wandering in deserts and mountains and caves and holes in the ground.* **AND ALL OF THESE,** *having gained approval through their faith,* **DID NOT RECEIVE WHAT WAS PROMISED,** *because God had provided something better for us, so that they would not be made perfect.*
> ~Hebrews 11:36-40 emphasis mine

These verses do not negate the idea of prosperity and success, but for me, undergirds that fact that no matter what happens, God is in control. I remember being in the Amazon jungle of Peru, and our leader, Bruce Coble, was teaching the tribe on covetousness. Hey, they did not have anything, but the head of the tribe told Bruce that this was a major problem in the village. When we left, they gave us a chicken, one of their most prized commodities. Fish were everywhere from the river, but they gave us the best they had. I am convinced that they experienced prosperity and success on a level that we never could realize.

GET THE CAN-DO ATTITUDE OF THE GO-GIVER

I can do all things through Him who strengthens me."
~Philippians 4:13

"Can't never did anything."

T he Can-Do attitude is an attitude that when faced with impossibilities you *"can do"* the impossible. We covered this secret in the previous secret and saw that the secret is not based on whatever circumstances and situations arise.

I Rodney Lewis Boyd (fill in your name) have strength for **ALL** *things (includes everything)* **IN CHRIST** *(the Anointed One and His anointing of yoke breaking, harassment removing, burden lifting, power of the Holy Ghost) who empowers me [I am ready for anything and equal to anything through Him who infuses inner strength into me; I am self-sufficient in Christ's sufficiency.*
~Philippians 4:13 Amplified Bible with emphasis,
additions, and commentary mine

People love to use this verse to describe the possibilities in every area of their lives and to be honest, I use this verse also, however, the context of the verse is the lessons learned about how not to speak from want (or need) and how to be content in whatever financial condition that he was in. Life is full of circumstances that range from one end of the spectrum to the other, financially.

Another aspect of the circumstance that Paul is speaking of is the fact that he was in prison for preaching the Gospel, and the church had revived their concern for him. He underscored that he did not need their money or the profit that he gained from their generosity. Remember that Philippians 4:14 is in the context of giving/receiving/money/wealth and the contentment when we do give.

I think another great secret is that when you *give*, then you *profit* by *increase* to your account.

Not that I (Paul) seek the gift (money) itself, but I seek for the profit which increases to your (the giver) account.
~Philippians 4:17

The law of cause and effect (giving and receiving) is "the law of laws" (Ralph Waldo Emerson).

"Don't give to receive, that is not giving but trading."
~Bob Proctor

Paul who had learned the secret of contentment and how to live in every and any circumstance, also had learned the secret of *giving* and yes, *receiving*. He had learned to *willingly give and graciously receive*.
~Bob Proctor

But I (Paul) have received everything in full (overflowing abundance); I am amply supplied having received from Ephaphroditus (who brought the gift) with what you have sent, a fragrant aroma, an acceptable sacrifice, well pleasing to God.
~Philippians 4:18 additions mine

Money that you give to someone else can be an *offering to your God*, that can have an aroma as much as an animal sacrificed to God. I love the smell of meat cooking on the grill. Your sacrifice wafts up to God and he breathes deep, and it is acceptable and well-pleasing to God. I am thinking that when you give to others, it is an act of faith since it pleases God.

And without faith (about your money) it is impossible to please Him (send up fragrant aroma that is an acceptable sacrifice) for he who comes to God for His provision, for He who comes to God must believe that He is a **REWARDER** *of those who seek Him and continues to seek Him.*

~Hebrews 11:6 with emphasis, additions, and commentary mine, Ruminator Style

When someone asked Bob Proctor if he was one of those Go-Getters, he replied, "No, I'm a Go-Giver."
Father God is the ultimate Go-Giver.

For God so loved (the motivation for His giving) that He **GAVE** *His only begotten/unique Son (Jesus) that whosoever* **BELIEVED** *(trusted in, clung to, relied on, adhered to, cleaved to) in Him (Jesus), should not perish* **BUT** *(in contrast) have everlasting, eternal life (not death).*

~John 3:16 with emphasis, additions, and commentary mine, Ruminator Style

-What motivated God's giving? (John 3:16)

-What/Who was God's gift that He gave? (John 3:16)

-For what purpose was God's gift? (John 3:16)

-Who was this gift for? (John 3:16)

-Who actually received the gift? (John 3:16)

NOTE: The gift was for everyone on planet earth from then until now **BUT** only those who **BELIEVED** (trusted in, clung to, relied on, adhered to, cleaved to) received.

*A **gift** opens the way and ushers **the giver** into the presence of the great.*
~Pro-Verbs 18:16

-What opens the way? (Pro-Verbs 18:16)

- Who is ushered into the presence of the great? (Pro-Verbs 18:16

For if the willingness is there, the gift is acceptable according to what one has, not according to what one does not have.
~2 Corinthians 8:12

-What is necessary for the gift to be acceptable? (2 Corinthians 8:12)

-What is this gift according to? (2 Corinthians 8:12)

*Give, and it will **be given** to you. A good measure, pressed down, shaken together, and running over, will be poured (will be given) into your lap. For with the measure, you use (give) it will be measured (given back) to you.*
~Luke 6:38 emphasis and addition mine

This verse is the primary verse on reciprocity, giving and receiving, seedtime and harvest Some would say, "we don't give to get." Some are **WRONG.** Hey, Jesus is the one who said, **GIVE** and it will be **GIVEN TO YOU,** so blame Jesus if you have a problem with giving to get.

-What will happen when you give? (Luke 6:38)

-What is the progressive nature of this "given to you?"

A **GOOD MEASURE** means that it is fair. It is not lacking. It is **GOOD.**
PRESSED DOWN is down to make room for **MORE.**
Being **SHAKEN TOGETHER** is to let things settle to **MAKE ROOM FOR MORE,** like when a box of cornflakes settles during shipping and a big box is only half full.
RUNNING OVER the top. This is called **ABUNDANCE,** an **OVERFLOW.**

NOTE: These four areas were started by the one who **GAVE** to **GET**.

-Who will give into your bosom/lap/receptacle for receiving what you get because your gave?

NOTE: Notice that it is **NOT** God who is giving to you, although we know that it is from God, but God uses other human beings, fish, ravens, etc. to supply your needs.

-How will the standard of measure be? (Luke 6:38)

Honor the Lord with your wealth, with the firstfruits of all your crops.
                                                        ~Pro-Verbs 3:9

-What are you to honor the Lord with? (Pro-Verbs 3:9)

-What part of your crops (or you paycheck) are you to honor the Lord with? (Pro-Verbs 3:9)

But you shall remember the Lord your God, for it is He who is giving you the power to make wealth.
                                                        ~Deuteronomy 8:18

-Who is giving you the power to make wealth? (Deuteronomy 8:18)

NOTE: Deuteronomy 8:2–17 speaks of the Lord's provision in the wilderness. Here are but a few things that God did/provided for them in the wilderness.
- He led them in the wilderness for 40 years.
- He allowed them to be hungry as He tested them to know what was in their hearts.
- He supplied manna (aka what is it, a thin, sweet bread) so they would know that man does not live by bread alone.

- Clothing did not wear out on them.
- Their feet did not swell (even though they were walking around for 40 years).
- He was bringing them into good land.
- The land had books of water, fountains, spring flowing forth in valleys and hills.
- It was a land of wheat, barley, vines, fig trees, pomegranates, olives oil, honey.
- It was a land where they ate food without scarcity, they would not lack anything
- It was a land whose stones are iron, and copper was in the hills to be dug out.
- They would eat, be satisfied.
- They would build good houses and live in them.
- Their herds and flocks will multiply.
- They had the potential to have hard, proud hearts and forget where the Lord delivered them
- He led them through the great and terrible wilderness with fiery serpents, scorpions and thirsty ground where there is no water.
- He supplied water from the rock of flint.
- Fed them manna.

Why would he do these things?

Otherwise, you may say in your heart, ***MY POWER AND THE STRENGTH OF MY HAND MADE ME THIS WEALTH.***
~Deuteronomy 8:17 emphasis mine

We must remember and never forget:

But you shall **REMEMBER** *that the Lord your God, for it is HE who is giving you (on a continual basis)* **POWER TO MAKE WEALTH**, *that He may confirm His covenant which He swore to your fathers, as it is this day."*
~Deuteronomy 8:18 emphasis and addition mine

So many times in this world, in this **RAT RACE**, we think we win under our own power, but all we are is the # 1 Rat, and that is not prosperity and success. The secret is to know who HE IS and who you **ARE NOT.**

Now He who supplies seed to the sower and bread for food will also supply and increase your store of seed and enlarge the harvest of your righteousness.

~2 Corinthians 9:10

-Who supplies seed to the sower? (2 Corinthians 9:10)

-What does He supply bread for? (2 Corinthians 9:10)

-What will he also supply and increase? (2 Corinthian 9:10)

-What will be enlarged? (2 Corinthians 9:10)

You will be enriched in every way (everything) so that you can be generous on every occasion, and through us your generosity will result in thanksgiving to God.

~2 Corinthians 9:11 addition mine

-In how many ways will you be enriched? (2 Corinthians 9:11)

-Why will you be enriched in every way (everything) ? (2 Corinthians 9:11)

-What will be the result in this enrichment and generosity? (2 Corinthians 9:11)

And God is able to bless you abundantly (make all grace abound) , so that in all things at all times, having all that you need (having all sufficiency), you will abound in every good work/deeds.

~2 Corinthians 9:8 addition mine

-Who is able to bless you abundantly? (2 Corinthians 9:8

-Why is God blessing you abundantly? (2 Corinthians 9:8)

-What will you have? (2 Corinthians 9:8)

Do not withhold good from those to whom it is due, when it is in your power to act.

~Pro-Verbs 3:27

-What should you not withhold? (Pro-Verbs 3:27)

-When should you not withhold from those to whom it is due? (Pro-Verbs 3:27)

Bring the whole tithe into the storehouse, that there may be food I my house. Test me in this, says the Lord Almighty, and see if I will not throw open the floodgates (windows) of heaven and pour out so much blessing that there will not be room enough to store it.

~Malachi 3:10 addition mine

-How much of the tithe should you bring into the storehouse? (Malachi 3:10)

-Why should you bring your whole tithe into the storehouse? (Malachi 3:10)

NOTE: A tithe is 1/10th of your income (what comes in). Some say when you add up all the various tithes, that it is 30%.

-What does God tell us to do in reference to bringing the whole tithe into the storehouse?

-What will God pour out on you when you test Him in the tithe? (Malachi 3:10)

-What will we see when we test God in the tithe? (Malachi 3:10)

-What will there not be when you test God on the tithe? (Malachi 3:10)

NOTE: Once again, we see the principle that when you **GIVE** you **GET,** and NOT just trickle-down economics, but full blown **FLOODGATES.** I think Jesus got this principle of reciprocity from Malachi 3:10)

NOTE TO THE NOTE: I believe that tithing is an Old Testament Principle. I also believe that we have been released from the tithe and now we are into the **GIVING** as a cheerful (hilarious) giver.

> *Let each one do as he as purposed (freely made the decision to give) in his heart/mind; not grudgingly or under compulsion; for God loves a cheerful (hilarious) giver.*
> ~2 Corinthians 9:7 additions mine

While I believe that we are released from the tithe into giving, I am not opposed to tithing. I believe that the tithe is a good starting point that leads into a spirit of generosity in giving. **IF** you are quibbling about how much you should give, then you have an Ananias and Sapphira heart. (Acts 5:1–11) I know people who do not tithe, but they give hilariously and outrageously and far exceed the amount of a tithe in their giving. Purpose in your heart what to give.

> *So when you give to the needy, do not announce it with trumpets, as the hypocrites do in the synagogues and on the streets, to be honored by others. Truly I tell you, they have received their reward in full.*
> ~Matthew 6:2

-How are we **NOT** to *give* to the needy? (Matthew 6:2)

-Who calls attention to how much you are giving? (Matthew 6:2)

-Why do the hypocrites give this way? (Matthew 6:2)

-What have they received in this kind of giving? (Matthew 6:2)

> *Give to everyone who asks you, and if anyone takes what belongs to you, do not demand it back.*
>> ~Luke 6:30

-What should you do to those who ask you to give to them? (Luke 6:30)

-What should you do to anyone who takes what belongs to you? (Luke 6:30)

-In this giving, how should you treat people? (Luke 6:31)

> *Take delight (delight yourself) in the Lord and He will give you the desires of your heart.*
>> ~Psalm 37:4 addition mine

-What should you take in the Lord? (Psalm 37:4)

-What will God do when you delight yourself (become pliable to him like clay in the potters hand? (Psalm 37:4)

> *All day long he craves for more, but the righteous give without sparing.*
>> ~Pro-Verbs 21:26

-What does the proud, haughty, scoffers who acts with insolent pride, and the sluggard refuse to do? (Pro-Verbs 21:24–25)

- What does the proud, haughty, scoffers who acts with insolent pride, and the sluggard do? (Pro-Verbs 21:26)

-What does the righteous do? (Pro-Verbs 21-26)

For even when we were with you, we used to give this order: IF anyone will not (chooses not to) work **NEITHER LET HIM EAT**. *For we hear that* **SOME** *among you are leading an undisciplined life,* **DOING NO WORK AL ALL**, *but acting like busybodies. Now* **SUCH PERSONS** *we command and exhort in the name Jesus Christ* **TO WORK** *in quiet fashion and eat their own bread. But as for you brethren, do not grow weary in doing good. And if anyone does not obey our instruction in this letter, take special note of that man and do not associate with him, so that he may be put to shame. And yet (at the same time) do not regard him as an enemy but admonish him as a brother.*

~1 Thessalonians 3:10–15 additions and emphasis mine

NOTE: In today's world there are many people who live off of the system, not working, always with a handout, living with a **WELFARE MENTALITY/PARADIGM,** who take and take and take and keep on taking without every lifting a hand to help themselves. At the same time there are many people who really are down and need a helping hand (with some money in that hand).

I believe that now more than ever that Christians need to be operating in the "gifts of the Spirit" one of which is the "discerning/distinguishing of spirits (human and/or demonic)."

(1 Corinthians 12:10) Paul Clark (pioneer musician in the Jesus Movement of the '70s) has a song that speaks of this in his song *Aim For The Heart.* I highly recommend checking it out.

Jesus answered, If you want to be perfect, go, sell your possessions, and give to the poor, and you will have treasure in heaven. Then come and follow me.

~Matthew 19:21

-What is the ultimate way to have treasures in heaven? (Matthew 19:21)

-After you (1) go (2) sell your possessions (3) give to the poor what is the next two-part step? (Matthew 19:21)

NOTE: This command was to the ones following him and not a mandate for every believer to do this. Ananias and Saphira sold their land and kept back a portion and acted like they gave all the proceeds to the poor, but they lied. Peter's response was:

> *But Peter said, Ananias, why has satan filled your heart to lie to the Holy Spirit, and to keep back some of the price of the land? While it remained unsold,* **DID IT NOT REMAIN YOUR OWN?** *And after it was sold,* **WAS IT NOT UNDER YOUR CONTROL...?**
>
> ~Act 5:3–4 emphasis mine

Many times we read of things that happened in the Bible and we try to make it a doctrine, like selling your property or meeting in homes, and those traditions end up "nullifying the Word of God." (Mark 7:13, Colossians 2:8)

> "Action done under wrong motives makes the actions wrong."
>
> ~Rodfucious

> *If I give all I possess to the poor and give over my body to hardship that I may boast, but do not have love, I gain nothing."*
>
> ~1 Corinthians 13:3

-What do you gain if you **GIVE ALL** you possess to the poor, or give over your body to hardship (suffer for the Lord) IF you don't have love? (1 Corinthians 13:3)

> *The wicked borrow and do not repay, but the righteous give generously.*
>
> ~Psalm 37:21

-What do the wicked **NOT** do when they borrow? (Psalm 37:21)

-How do the righteous give? (Psalm 37:21)

Heal the sick, raise the dead, cleanse those who have leprosy, drive out demons. Freely you have received; freely give.
         ~Matthew 10:8

-When you (not if you) heal the sick, raise the dead, cleanse those who have leprosy and drive out demons, what should you charge? (Mark 10:8)

NOTE: This does not mean that you can't receive money or goods. Paul states that, "a laborer is worthy of his hire" (Luke 10:7) and "You shall not muzzle an ox while it treads out the grain/corn and the laborer is worthy of his hire." (1 Timothy 5:18) Other verses includes

Matthew 10:10, Leviticus 19:13, Deuteronomy 24:15) Paul wrote in prison to those who gave him stuff/money, that he didn't need their money, but he accepted it for **THEIR SAKES**, for how they would benefit from giving. I am retired, but I still teach, write books, counsel etc. I give books away, but I also sell my books. Some would say, the Gospel is free, but I say that, yes, the Gospel is free but printing costs. Part of my financial policy is, (1) a laborer is worthy of his hire (2) You pray and then you obey by giving me whatever the Lord lays on your heart. IF he does not lay on your heart to give me anything, then don't give me anything.

But when you give to the needy, do not let your left hand know what your right hand is doing, so that your giving may be in secret. Then your Father, who sees what is done in secret will reward you.
         ~Matthew 6:3–4

-What should you do or not do when you give to the needy? (Matthew 6:3)

-How should your giving be done? (Matthew 6:3)

-What will happen when the Father sees what is done in secret? (Matthew 6:3)

Some religious people will point to this verse as you should never allow any of your generous giving to be seen in public. The context of this verse is for people who **PRACTICE THEIR RIGHTOUS-NESS** before men for the purpose of being **NOTICED BY THEM.** Some of the self-righteous givers sounded trumpets in the synagogues and streets so that men may honor them. (Matthew 6:7–8) It is all about the attitude of the heart. I believe (I think I'm right, but I could be wrong) that giving is good and praying is good in public. Jesus was praying once in public in the midst of mourners at a grave site (a tomb site) for Lazarus to be raised from the dead (Jesus delayed coming to Mary and Martha while Lazarus was sick). Lazarus died, he was three days in the tomb, and he stunk. (Read John 11:1–57 for full details)

> *And so they removed the stone. And Jesus raised His eyes, and* **SAID**, *Father; I thank Thee that Thou heard Me (past tense). And I knew that Thou heard Me always; BUT because of the* **PEOPLE STANDING AROUND I SAID IT (out loud in their presence)** *that (the reason for not praying in a closet)* **THAT THEY MAY BELIEVE THAT THOU DID SENT ME.**
> ~John 11:41–42 emphasis and additions mine

It is all about the attitude of your heart.

> *Remember this: Whoever sows sparingly will also reap sparingly, and whoever sows generously will also reap generously.*
> ~2 Corinthians 9:6

-What will happen when someone sows (gives money/seeds) sparingly? (2 Corinthians 9:6)

-What will happen when someone sows (gives money/seeds) generously? (2 Corinthians 9:6)

Over and over and over again we see throughout the Scriptures that we have a mandate to **BE GO-GIVERS** so we can become **GO-GETTERS/RECEIVERS.** The problem arises when all we do is give nothing and expect something for nothing. The **SECRET OF SUCCESS** is give, give, give and you will get, get, get.

GET LINKED TO THE STRENGTH & SUPPLY CHAIN

I can do all things through Christ Who strengthens me.
                                        ~Philippians 4:13

And my God will supply all your needs according to His riches in glory in Christ Jesus.
                                        ~Philippians 4:19

At the time of this writing, there is a chink in the chain of supply and demand. There are multiple reasons from the coronavirus to world events like Russia dominating the weaker Ukraine, to political unrest, to lack of workers, to a recession, etc. During the '70s there was a thing called "trickledown economics" where the money went from the top and trickled down and by the time it reaches the bottom tier there was not much left. There are always reasons which turn into excuses for trusting systems versus trusting God.

In God's Pro-Vison there is **STRENGTH AND SUPPLY.** The key to prosperity (having enough to meeting your needs and an overflow to help others) and success (accomplishing the purposes of God in your life) to get "linked to the chain" of the **STRENGTH AND SUPPLY CHAIN.**

*I have **STRENGTH** for all things in Christ (the Anointed One and His anointing) Who **EMPOWERS** me [I am ready for anything and equal to anything through Him Who **INFUSES INNER STRENGTH** into me; I am **SELF-SUFFICIENT** in **CHRIST'S SUFFICIENCY.***

~Philippians 4:13 Amplified Bible with emphasis, additions and commentary mine, Ruminator Style

- **I HAVE:** This means that I already have, not that I'm going to get. It is a spiritual fact that the Holy Ghost dwells inside of me and that by faith I have access to all things that I could think or ask because of Christ (the Anointed One and His anointing that dwells in me so I can have the hope (confident expectation of glory).
- **STRENGTH:** *force* (literally or figuratively); specifically miraculous *power* (usually by implication a *miracle* itself): - ability, abundance, meaning, might (-ily, -y, -y deed), (worker of) miracle (-s), power, strength, violence, mighty (wonderful) work.

STRENGTHEN: endunamoō (*en-doo-nam-o'-o*)= to *empower:* - enable, (increase in) strength (-en), be (make) strong.

There is empowerment and an enablement in a world of weakness and powerlessness to do anything about the world economy.
- **FOR ALL THINGS:** *All includes all.* The context is for Pro-Vision/money, but I believe that it will include any and everything in our lives.
- **IN CHRIST:** Christ means the Anointed One (Jesus) who has been anointed by God with power, dynamic ability (strength), the yoke breaking, burden lifting, harassing and oppression removing, healing power of the Holy Ghost.
- **WHO EMPOWERS/STRENGTHENS ME:** The Anointed One with His anointing gives us strength and ability, an enablement to accomplish His purposes in our lives

Whatever we face in life, good, bad, or ugly, our secret weapon to help us face anything is The Anointed One and His anointing. This anointing is found within us, within our human spirit, the lamp of the Lord, as "Christ in you the hope (confident expectation) of glory (the light and presence of God)." (Colossians 1:27)

Take some time and memorize Philippians 4:14 and 4:19 and let/allow your mind to dwell on these two verses instead of the 24 hour negative news cycle.

TAP IN TO THE AUTHORITY OF WORDS

*Death and life are in **the power of the tongue,** and those who love it will eat its fruit.*

~Pro-Verbs 18:21 emphasis mine

POWER: yâd (*yawd)*=A primitive word; **a *hand* (the *open* one (indicating *power, means, direction*, etc.),** in distinction from H3709, the *closed* one); used (as noun, adverb, etc.) in a great variety of applications, both literally and figuratively, both proximate and remote: - (+ be) able, X about, + armholes, at, axletree, because of, beside, border, X bounty, + broad, [broken-] handed, X by, charge, coast, + consecrate, + creditor, custody, debt, dominion, X enough, + fellowship, force, X from, hand [-staves, -y work], X he, himself, X in, labour, + large, ledge, [left-] handed, means, X mine, ministry, near, X of, X order, ordinance, X our, parts, pain, power, X presumptuously, service, side, sore, state, stay, draw with strength, stroke, + swear, terror, X thee, X by them, X them-selves, X thine own, X thou, through, X throwing, + thumb, times, X to, X under, X us, X wait on, [way-] side, where, + wide, X with (him, me, you), work, + yield, X your-selves.

Words are powerful things. In the beginning, words were used in the creative process. Words are merely thoughts expressed.

*Then God **SAID** (expressed His thoughts and desires verbally), Let (allow it to happen) there be light (the thought of God)...*

~Genesis 1:3,
emphasis and additions mine

The cause and effect of the expressed thoughts of God was, "… and there was light."

We are created beings with the blueprint being created in "the image and likeness of God".

(Genesis 1:26-27, Genesis 2:7, Genesis 2:21–25) I believe that one of *the secrets to success* is the dynamic that we were created in the image and likeness of God which includes *creativity* and *power words*.

When we speak our thoughts out loud, we are setting into motion the creative process for good, bad, and ugly.

As a man thinketh in his heart/mind so he is.
~Pro-Verbs 27:3

*…out of the **abundance (overflow)** of the heart/mind the mouth speaks.*
~Luke 6:45

In the physical when we speak, someone hears. Our thoughts are encoded (processed to send out) and decoded (processed what we hear). As we speak our thoughts out, someone hears our words. Our vocal folds have a certain frequency and vibration, and the ears (the hearing mechanism) also has a certain frequency and vibration) that goes to the brain via the VIII Cranial Nerve (the acoustic nerve). Our powerful words goes out to God Himself, to the d-evil/demons, to other human beings, to ourselves, to creation itself including the animals, and even the trees, the rocks, to the created universe, and to any of God's creation.

There is cause and effect when our words are expressed.

Death and life *are in the **power of the tongue**, and those who love it and indulge it **will eat its fruit and bear the consequences of their words.***
~Pro-Verbs 18:21 Amplified Bible, emphasis mine

The tongue is merely the extension of the mind. It is the tongue that can control our lives, but it is still just an extension the mind, what we think.

> *For we stumble in many ways. IF anyone does not stumble IN WHAT HE SAYS, he is a perfect man, able to bridle the whole body as well. Now if we put the bits into the horses MOUTHS so that they may obey us, we direct their entire body as well.*
>
> ~James 3:2–3, emphasis mine

Your words can entrap you or free you. The mouth/tongue is the revealer of the mind/heart, while the bridle is our free will/choice at taking control/authority over what we think and say.

> *Behold, the ships also, though they are so great and are driven by strong winds, are still* **DIRECTED** *by a very small rudder (the tongue) wherever the inclination of the pilot (that would be you) desires.*
>
> ~James 3:4, emphasis and additions mine

You life will either be on course, or your faith will be shipwrecked (1 Timothy 1:18–19) depending on your tongue, what you speak.

The tongue, once again, is not what is in control of your ship (life), it is what you *think* that is what is *expressed from your mouth* that determines your life. Pro-Verbs 23:7 is so true, "As a man, woman, human **THINKS** so they are." (Pro-Verbs 23:7) Combine that with Luke 6:45:

> *Out of the abundance/overflow of the heart/mind (what you think) the* **MOUTH** *(where the tongue is located)* **SPEAKS** *(expresses your thoughts that determine your world.*
>
> ~Luke 6:45, emphasis and addition mine

> *And the tongue is a small part of the body, and yet it boasts of great things (good, bad, ugly). Behold how great a forest is set aflame by such a small fire! And the tongue is a fire, the very world of iniquity; the tongue is set among our members as that which defiles the entire*

body, and sets on fire the **COURSE OF OUR LIFE,** *and is set on fire by hell (Gehenna, a garbage dump that burns perpetually outside of Jerusalem).*

~James 3:6, additions and emphasis mine

Tongue power is under your control. You have as part of your soul, your mind (what you think) your volition (your free will) and your emotions (the barometer of your feelings. You tongue can dictate to you if you are happy or sad or depressed, anxious, fearful, etc. This in turn affects your physical being (which your tongue is part of).

We are an interconnected being according to I Thessalonians 5:23.

Now, may the God of peace Himself sanctify you entirely; and may your spirit (the lamp of the Lord, the core of who you are) and soul (your mind/what you think), you will/what you choose to do, and your emotions/the barometer of your feelings) be preserved compete, without blame at the coming of our Lord Jesus Christ.

~1 Thessalonians 5:23 with emphasis, additions, commentary mine, Ruminator Style

The tongue is an extension of our thoughts, much like our body are an instrument of unrighteousness or righteousness. The use of the body, including the tongue can be used for good or be used for the bad and ugly depending on your presentation. (Romans 6:12–14)

DEATH: mâveth (*maw'-veth)*=From H4191; *death* (natural or violent); concretely the *dead*, their place or state (*hades*); figuratively *pestilence, ruin:* - (be) dead ([-ly]), death, die (-d)

H4191: mûth (*mooth)*=A primitive root; to *die* (literally or figuratively); causatively to *kill:* - X at all, X crying, (be) dead (body, man, one), (put to, worthy of) death, destroy (-er), (cause to, be like to, must) die, kill, necro [-mancer], X must needs, slay, X surely, X very suddenly, X in [no] wise.

LIFE: chay (*khah'ee)*=From H2421; *alive;* hence *raw* (flesh); *fresh*

(plant, water, year), *strong*; also (as noun, especially in the feminine singular and masculine plural) *life* (or living thing), whether literally or figuratively: - + age, alive, appetite, (wild) beast, company, congregation, life (-time), live (-ly), living (creature, thing), maintenance, + merry, multitude, + (be) old, quick, raw, running, springing, troop. **H2421: châyâh** (*khaw-yaw'*)=A prim root (compare H2331, H2424); to *live*, whether literally or figuratively; causatively to *revive:* - keep (leave, make) alive, X certainly, give (promise) life, (let, suffer to) live, nourish up, preserve (alive), quicken, recover, repair, restore (to life), revive, (X God) save (alive, life, lives), X surely, be whole.

Death and life are like the choice of blessing/life or curse/death. (Deuteronomy 30:19–20)

Our words are the expression of our *mind* set. Our *mind* set is created by what we *set our minds on* and *what we think and say to and about ourselves and about others and situations and circumstances in our lives.*

> *The mind set (a verb, our focus, what we think about creating our mindset) on the flesh (carnal nature, d-evil thoughts, the world's thoughts, negativity) is* **DEATH**, *but (in contrast to) the mind set (a verb, our focus, what we think about creating our mindset) on the Spirit (the Holy Spirit, the Word of God, the things of God, positivity) is* **LIFE** *(and that more abundant) and* **PEACE** *(wholeness, rest, no stress, no anxiety, worry, fear, tension).*
>
> ~Romans 8:6 with emphasis, additions,
> and commentary mine, Ruminator Style

THOSE WHO LOVE IT: âhab 'âhêb (*aw-hab', aw-habe'*)=A primitive root; to *have affection* for (sexually or otherwise): - (be-) love (-d, -ly, -r), like, friend.

This affection can be for the words of life or the words of death will determine your R.A.M. which is your results, achievements, manifestations (good, bad or ugly).

WILL EAT: âkal (*aw-kal'*)=A primitive root; to *eat* (literally or figuratively): - X at all, burn up, consume, devour (-er, up), dine, eat (-er, up), feed (with), food, X freely, X in . . . wise (-deed, plenty), (lay) meat, X quite.

If you eat food, you will either be nourished, or you will be malnourished. You can eat food and be satisfied, or you can eat food and have heartburn, be nauseous and throw up. The is true with the words that you consume, positive or negative, godly, or ungodly, life or death. It is hinged on what you choose to eat.

ITS FRUIT: perîy (*per-ee'*)=From H6509; *fruit* (literally or figuratively): - bough, ([first-]) fruit ([-ful]), reward. **H6509: pârâh (*paw-raw'*)**=A primitive root; to *bear fruit* (literally or figuratively): - bear, bring forth (fruit), (be, cause to be, make) fruitful, grow, increase.

Fruit is the outcome of the harvest. Fruit can be luscious (life) or rotten (death). What we plant with our mouth will determine the outcomes, the results, the manifestations in our lives. When you study Mark 4:1-20, the parable of the Kingdom about the Seed, Soil and Sower, you can see the power over the Seed/Word, as powerful as it is, can be choked out, drived up.

What you are thinking, what you are speaking and what you are doing creates the outcomes in our lives. Learn the secrets of the power of your words.

I love the book of **PRO-VERBS**, the book of **PRO=POSITIVE/ VERBS=ACTIONS** for living a practical life. Here is some wise advice concerning your words

> "**IF** *you have been foolish in exalting yourself* **OR** *if you have plotted evil,* **PUT YOUR HAND ON YOUR MOUTH.** *For the churning of milk produces butter, and pressing the nose brings forth blood; SO the churning of anger produces strife.*
> ~Pro-Verbs 30:32–33, emphasis mine

Let's extrapolate Pro-Verbs 30:32–33.

- **IF YOU HAVE BEEN FOOLISH IN EXALTING YOUR-SELF:** We can be foolish. That foolishness exalts us in our own minds, what we think. "The fool has said in his own heart that there is **NO** God." (Psalm 14:1, Psalm 51:1) The only thing worse is a Christian who acts like there is **NO** God."
- **OR IF YOU HAVE PLOTTED EVIL:** Exaltation and plotting evil start in the mind and is manifested by our words coming out of our **MOUTH.** There is a practical positive action that we can take.
- **PUT YOUR HAND ON YOUR MOUTH:** Wow! The power of your free will can stop your thoughts in their tracks from ever coming out of your mouth. Remember the mouth, your words are the great revealer of your heart/mind.
- **FOR THE CHURNING OF MILK PRODUCES BUTTER:** You mouth is the butter churn. The speaking of your words is the agitator, and the butter is the outcome of your thoughts/words being spoken over and over and over and over again.
- **AND THE PRESSING OF THE NOSE BRINGS FORTH BLOOD:** Again, the agitation of your body/nose has a cause and effect and that cause, and effect is a bloody nose.
- **SO THE CHURNING OF ANGER PRODUCES STRIFE:** The Word says that "whatever a man sows that shall he also reap." (Galatians 6:7) I believe that it can be said that "whatever a man churns/presses/agitates, that shall he also reap and produce."

Picture a butter churn and then picture your mouth. In the churn/your heart/your mouth/your mind are negative thoughts. Now picture your **TONGUE** as the agitator that goes up and down over and over and over and over again. The cause and effect is production of either butter or in the cause of pressing the nose, blood **OR** thinking about and talking about what makes you angry produces **STRIFE.** It is what is in the churn that determines what is produced.

I am an Elvis fan, and he had a hit with a song called **BURN-ING LOVE.** I imagine that if you replaced anger with love, then you would have a *hunka-hunk of churning love.* Yes, I went there and said it, and no, I do not apologize.

The bottom line about this secret of success is that you have the authority and dynamic ability to choose your words and shape your destiny.

THE POWER OF PREPARATION

Then Joshua said to the people, consecrate yourself (today) for tomorrow the Lord will do wonders among you.
~Joshua 3:5, addition mine

Many moons ago, I was in a Bible College/University taking a class in homiletics (how to prepare a sermon and present it). The professor was a crusty old curmudgeon. The first words out of his mouth on the first day of class was, "You young preacher boys, you think that you will open your mouth and the Lord will fill it... **YEAH WITH HOT AIR!** You've got to study to show yourself approved." He was saying that you have to *prepare* your sermon before you preach it.

Many people approach life just accepting whatever happens. They are like Doris Day who sings, "Que, Sera, Sera." Some say, "Oh well, whatever happens, happens." The difference between successful people and failures is *preparation or lack of preparation.*

The children of Israel were released from slavery in Egypt with the purpose to go into the Promised Land. What was supposed to be an 11-day journey turned into a 40-year fiasco. (Deuteronomy 1:2-5) After 40 years of going around the same mountain, Moses spoke to the children.

The Lord our God spoke to us at Horeb, saying you have **STAYED LONG ENOUGH** *at this mountain.* **TURN** *and* **SET** *you journey (turn on your G.P.S, God's Positioning System) and* **GO** *(break your pattern and go in a different direction) to the hill country* *of the Amorites, and to all their neighbors in the Arabah, in the hill country and in the lowland and in the Negev and by the seacoast the land of the Canaanites, and Lebanon, as fare as the great river, the river Euphrates.*

~Deuteronomy 1:6–7, Numbers 13:1–29
emphasis and addition mine

"See, I have placed the **LAND** *before you: (1) Go in (2) and possess the land which the Lord swore to give to your fathers, to Abraham, to Isaac, and to Jacob, to them and their descendants after them."*
~Deuteronomy 1:8 emphasis and addition mine

NOTE: This was the original plan 40 years earlier. There may be some dreams, goal, vision, imagination that you thought was derailed and will never be accomplished in your life. The secret is that you may have wasted many years by sin, rebellion, fear etc., **BUT** it is never too late to cross over and possess your desires, dreams, visions, imaginations, **BUT** you must be prepared.

1. You must prepare to be *"strong and courageous"* because you will have every opportunity to be *"weak and discouraged."* (Deuteronomy 31:6, Deuteronomy 31:7, Deuteronomy 31:23, Joshua 1:6, Joshua 1:7, Joshua 1:9, Joshua 1:18, Joshua 10:25)
2. Do not *"tremble or be dismayed"* because you will have every opportunity to shake in your boots and have cause to lose courage or resolution, be alarmed and fearful and upset. (Joshua 1:9)
3. *Prepare provisions* for yourselves, for within three days you are to cross this Jordan, to go in and possess the land which the Lord your God is giving you to possess it. (Joshua 1:11)

NOTE: In the natural, provision would be water, food, weaponry, armor, tents/shelter, etc. In the spiritual I believe that preparation of provision would include, the living waters/The Holy Spirit, food/The Word of God/The Sword of God, the armor of God, the Name of the Lord a strong tower, etc.

Keep the Promise/Covenant/God's Word before you. (Genesis 1:1–3, Romans 4:13-25)

> *Then Joshua said to the people,* **consecrate yourself** *(today) for tomorrow* **the Lord will do wonders** *among you.*
> ~Joshua 3:5 emphasis and addition mine

SANCTIFY/CONSECRATE qâdash (*kaw-dash'*)=A primitive root; to *be* (causatively *make, pronounce* or *observe* as) *clean* (ceremonially or morally): - appoint, bid, consecrate, dedicate, defile, hallow, (be, keep) holy (-er, place), keep, prepare, proclaim, purify, sanctify (-ied one, self), X wholly.

NOTE: We know that God is the great sanctifier/consecrator, however we see in Joshua 3:5 that we are the ones called to do the sanctifying/consecrating. We know that "faith without corresponding actions (works/deeds that we do) is dead/of none effect." (James 2:17) In all of our preparation, be prepared to do something. The children of Israel were promised a land, but *they still had to go in and possess it.* I believe that when we "consecrate ourselves" we are positioning ourselves for God to consecrate/sanctify us.

NOTE TO THE NOTE: The implied meaning of "consecrate yourself" is to consecrate yourself (prepare yourself) **TODAY** (before tomorrow before you go in to possess the land).

FOR TOMORROW THE LORD WILL DO WONDERS AMONG YOU:

WONDERS: pâlâ' (*paw-law'*)=A primitive root; properly perhaps to *separate,* that is, *distinguish* (literally or figuratively); by implication to *be* (causatively *make*) *great, difficult, wonderful:* - accomplish, (arise . . . too, be too) hard, hidden, things too high, (be, do, do a, shew) marvelous (-ly, -els, things, work), miracles, perform, separate, make singular, (be, great, make) wonderful (-ers, -ly, things, works), wondrous (things, works, -ly).

NOTE: Signs and wonders are merely signs of how wonderful God is . I usually write, "Wonderful, full of wonder). When you are prepared, you will not miss out on how wonderful, full of wonder that God is. All you will be able to do is to "scratch your head and wonder, how did he do that?

When you are prepared in your life, in your business, in your personal relationships, things will not sneak up on you and take you by surprise. Oh, things will happen when you least expect it but if you are prepared, you will have a contingency plan. So, plan on purpose, plan with a purpose. Plan on purpose for the purpose o success. You will get exactly what you plan.

WALK IN PROSPERITY

*Beloved, I pray (wish) that in all respects you may **prosper** and be in good health, just as your soul prospers.*
~3 John 2 addition and emphasis mine

Many people believe that John is writing to someone, and this verse is merely an opening greeting to the person, like dear so and so. That may well be, however I believe John is expressing his true desire to his "beloved Gaius," that he would prosper.

Biblical prosperity is not just and accumulation of wealth to hoard and consume on our own lust, but it is, "having enough to meet your needs (not your greed) and an overflow to help others. True Biblical prosperity is for every area of your life, financial, health and prospering in your soul (in your mind what you think, your free will what you choose, and your emotions the barometer of your feelings).

We have seen in **SECRETS TO SUCCESS # 2 LEARN THE ART OF MEDITATION,** that prosperity and success in hinged on meditating (contemplating, pondering, pondering, thinking, thought, deliberation) of the Word of God/The Law/The Principles of prosperity and success. (Joshua 1:8)

BELOVED: agapētos (*ag-ap-ay-tos'*)=From G25; *beloved:* - (dearly, well) beloved, dear. =Perhaps from ἄγαν agan (*much*; or compare [H5689]); to *love* (in a social or moral sense): - (be-) love (-ed).

NOTE: This love for the beloved is the same love (agape') that God has for the world, for you and the same type of love that we should have for God, the same type of love that we should have for one another, which can only take place when you have love for yourself. It is hard to love the ones (you and your neighbors) when you hate the ones that "God so loved". I believe that if God was saying this to us, his beloved, that God would say, "Rodney (fill in your name) I speak forth to you prosperity in your finances and good health and soul prosperity." The d-evil would say, "Rodney, (fill in your name), I wish for you poverty, sickness and soul sickness."

I PRAY/WISH: euchomai (*yoo'-khom-ahee)*=Middle voice of a primary verb; to *wish*; by implication to *pray* to God: - pray, will, wish.

NOTE: John is praying and wishing *good things*, not *bad things* for his friend. How much more does God want these things in our lives. God is a **GOOD GOD!**

ABOVE: peri (*per-ee')*= properly *through* (all *over*), that is, *around*; figuratively *with respect* to; used in various applications, of place, cause or time (with the genitive case denoting the *subject* or *occasion* or *superlative* point; with the accusative case the *locality, circuit, matter, circumstance* or general *period*In compounds it retains substantially the same meaning of circuit (*around*), excess (*beyond*), or completeness (*through*).

ALL THINGS: pas (*pas)*=Including all the forms of declension; apparently a primary word; *all, any, every,* the *whole:* - all (manner of, means) alway (-s), any (one), X daily, + ever, every (one, way), as many as, + no (-thing), X throughly, whatsoever, whole, whosoever.

NOTE: This shows how important the message was to prosper, and be in health, even as the soul prospers. It ranks above all other things for the life of the believer.

PROSPER: euodoō (*yoo-od-o'-o)*=From a compound of G2095 and G3598; to *help* on the *road*, that is, (passively) *succeed in reaching*; figuratively to *succeed* in business affairs: - (have a) prosper (-ous journey).

NOTE: To reach the goal of prosperity on the road to success is the goal for the journey.

BE (state of being) IN HEALTH: hugiainō (*hoog-ee-ah'ee-no*)=From G5199; to *have* sound *health*, that is, *be well* (in body); figuratively to be *uncorrupt* (*true* in doctrine): - be in health, (be safe and) sound, (be) whole (-some). G5199: hugiēs (*hoog-ee-ace'*)=From the base of G837; *healthy*, that is, *well* (in body); figuratively *true* (in doctrine): - sound, whole. G837: auxanō (*owx-an'-o*)=A prolonged form of a primary verb; to *grow* ("wax"), that is, *enlarge* (literally or figuratively, actively or passively): - grow (up), (give the) increase.

NOTE: Health is a state of being in the physical. To be sound and whole and to enlarge is our health is something we desire to be.

EVEN AS: kathōs (*kath-oce'*)=From G2596 and G5613; *just* (or *inasmuch*) *as, that:* - according to, (according, even) as, how, when.

NOTE: Prosperity in the areas of riches, health is on the same level as soul prosperity.

SOUL: psuchē (*psoo-khay'=*)From G5594; *breath,* that is, (by implication) *spirit,* abstractly or concretely (the *animal* sentient principle only; thus distinguished on the one hand from G4151, which is the rational and immortal *soul*; and on the other from G2222, which is mere *vitality,* even of plants: these terms thus exactly correspond respectively to the Hebrew [H5315], [H7307] and [H2416]: - heart (+ -ily), life, mind, soul, + us, + you.

NOTE: The mind (how and what we think), our free will choices based on a prosperous soul and our emotional stability is desired.

PROSPER: euodoō (*yoo-od-o'-o*)=From a compound of G2095 and G3598; to *help* on the *road,* that is, (passively) *succeed in reaching;* figuratively to *succeed* in business affairs

SOWING THE WHATEVER SEEDS

*Do not be deceived, God is not mocked; for whatever a man **sows**, this he will also **reap**.*

~Galatians 6:7 emphasis mine

One of the d-evil's deceptions is to believe that we can sow bad stuff and get away with it. People tend to live their lives as close to the riverbanks edge without slipping in. They believe that they can walk on the slippery slope and never "slip sliding away." This mentality violates the principles of sowing and reaping, seedtime and harvest, the laws of reciprocity.

"You can't live like hell and expect heaven results."

~Rodfucious

"You can't live in a curse and expect blessings."

~Rodfucious

"The person who sows seeds of poison ivy, should not be surprised when they develop a rash."

~Rodfucious

The Psalmist King writes about this in Psalm 37:1.

Do not fret because of evildoers (doers of evil, sowers of seeds of evil) be not envious of wrongdoers (doers of wrong, sowers of seeds of wrong).

~Psalm 37:1 addition mine

The question arises, "Why"? Why should we not fret or be envious of the seed sowers of evil and wrong? The answer is found in the next verse.

> *For they (the evil and wrong doers) will wither (cause and effect of sowing evil and wrong seeds) quickly like grass and fade like the green herb.*
>
> ~Psalm 37:2 addition mine

> *Do not be deceived (by what it looks like), God is not mocked (by the evildoers and wrongdoers), for whatever (no limit) a man (evildoer and wrongdoers) sows (plants), this he (evildoers and wrong doers) will also reap (get a harvest of what is sown).*
>
> ~Galatians 6:7 with emphasis, additions, and commentary mine, Ruminator Style

NOTE: Of course, this same principle *works for good sowing* also.

> *For the one who sows to his own flesh (the evil and wrong doers) will from the flesh reap corruption (wither quickly like grass and fade like the green herb)* **BUT** *(in contrast) the one who sows to the Spirit (the godly and right doers) reap eternal life (and that more abundantly).*
>
> ~Galatians 6:8 additions and emphasis mine

The seeds germinate (sprout, grow, develop) in our minds (what we think) and is planted by our words (mouth and tongue) and actions (what we do) into the soil (hearts) of this world. The seeds can be sown into another person, into the universe, into yourself with the cause and effect being the "whatever" principle being activated.

GOD IS NOT MOCKED

MOCKED: muktērizō (*mook'-tay-rid'-zo)*=From a derivative of the base of G3455 (meaning *snout*, as that whence *lowing* proceeds from); to *make mouths* at, that is, *ridicule:* - mock. **G3455: mukaomai (*moo-kah'-om-ahee*)**=From a presumed derivative of μύζω muzō (to "moo"); to *bellow* (*roar*): - roar.

> "Are you a mod or a rocker?" (Question to Ringo Starr when the came to America)
> "Neither, I'm a "mocker". (Ringo's answer)

We live in a world of mockers who take every opportunity that they can to put down, Christians and the God that Christians worship. In these dark dazes of being "woke" and "cancel culture" if you take a stand for God, you will be mocked for believe in God, who will also be mocked. If you believe that God is NOT against money, wealth, prosperity, and success, you will mocked as they declare that you are preaching the "Prosperity Gospel". There is really no "Prosperity Gospel" there is on the Gospel of the Death, Burial, Resurrection of Jesus. Of course there is nothing new under the sun, including talk about "another gospel." (Galatians 1:6–9)

WHATEVER

WHATEVER: ean (*eh-an'*)= a *conditional* particle; *in case* that, *provided*, etc.; often used in connection with other particles to denote *indefiniteness* or *uncertainty*: - before, but, except, (and) if, (if) so, (what-, whither-) soever, though, when (-soever), whether (or), to whom, [who-] so (-ever).

A MAN

MAN/HUMAN: anthrōpos (*anth'-ro-pos*)= the *countenance*; from G3700); *manfaced*, that is, a *human* being: - certain, man.

SOWS

SOWS: speirō (*spi'-ro*)=Probably strengthened from G4685 (through the idea of *extending*); to *scatter*, that is, *sow* (literally or figuratively): - sow (-er), receive seed. **G4685: spaō** (*spah'-o*)=A primary verb; to *draw:* - draw (out).

REAP: theridō (*ther-id'-zo*)=From G2330 (in the sense of the *crop*); to *harvest:* - reap. **G2330: theros** (*ther'-os*)=From a primary word θέρω therō (to *heat*); properly *heat*, that is, *summer:* - summer.

FOR THE ONE WHO SOWS (AKA THE SOWER)

SOWS: speirō (*spi'-ro*)=Probably strengthened from G4685 (through the idea of *extending*); to *scatter*, that is, *sow* (literally or figuratively): - sow (-er), receive seed. **G4685: spaō** (*spah'-o*)=A primary verb; to *draw:* - draw (out).

TO HIS OWN FLESH

FLESH: Sarx (*sarx*)= *flesh* (as *stripped* of the skin), that is, (strictly) the *meat* of an animal (as food), or (by extension) the *body* (as opposed to the soul (or spirit), or as the symbol of what is external, or as the means of kindred, or (by implication) *human nature* (with its frailties (physically or morally) and passions), or (specifically) a *human being* (as such): - carnal (-ly, + -ly minded), flesh ([-ly]).

You can have the human body flesh, you can have chili con carné, chili with meat, but the meaning of flesh in the case of a human being is the sinful nature of mankind. When you sow to the carnal nature they are sowing to 'his own flesh/nature). I believe that by our free will, that we can sow seeds of good to our flesh/nature. The harvest of sowing to the flesh/carnal nature is found in Galatians 5:19-21 which negates the Kingdom of God in the life. There will be no righteousness, peace and joy in the Holy Ghost. (Romans 14:17(

BUT

In contrast to sowing negative seed to the carnal nature.

THE ONE WHO SOWS TO THE SPIRIT

SPIRIT: Pneuma (*pnyoo'-mah*)=From G4154; a *current* of air, that is, *breath* (*blast*) or a *breeze*; by analogy or figuratively a *spirit*, that is, (human) the rational *soul*, (by implication) *vital principle*, mental *disposition*, etc., or (superhuman) an *angel*, *daemon*, or (divine) God, Christ's *spirit*, the Holy *spirit*: - ghost, life, spirit (-ual, -ually), mind. **G4154: pneō (*pneh'-o*)**=A primary word; to *breathe* hard, that is, *breeze*: - blow.

The sower, the human being (the spirit, the little s dwelling in the human body, the lamp of the Lord Pro-Verbs 20:27), can also sow to The Spirit (the Holy Spirit) which is manifested in the fruit of the Spirit found in Galatians 5:22–23)

SHALL FROM THE SPIRIT (Big S, The Holy Spirit) REAP ETERNAL LIFE

ETERNAL: aiōnios (*ahee-o'-nee-os*)=From G165; *perpetual* (also used of past time, or past and future as well): - eternal, for ever, everlasting, world (began). **G165: aiōn (*ahee-ohn'*)**= properly an *age*; by extension *perpetuity* (also past); by implication the *world*; specifically (Jewish) a Messianic period (present or future): - age, course, eternal, (for) ever (-more), [n-]ever, (beginning of the, while the) world (began, without end).

Eternal/Eternity/Everlasting life is a long time. It is hinged on your choice of seed.

LIFE: zōē (*dzo-ay*)=From G2198; *life* (literally or figuratively): - life (-time). **G2198: zaō (*dzah'-o*)**= primary verb; to *live* (literally or figuratively): - life (-time), (a-) live (-ly), quick.

As said before, life versus death is hinged on the choice of the seed that you sow and the choice of soil.

As with all of the natural laws/principles they are rooted in spiritual laws/principles and will determine having enough to meet your needs (not your greed) and an overflow to help others (prosperity) and accomplishing the purposes of God in your life and your possessions (success).

BE A VISIONARY

Without a vison, the people perish.

~Pro-Verbs 29:18

Without a revelatory vision the people are unrestrained.
~Pro-Verbs 29:18 translated from Spanish,
thanks and R.I.P Kirk DeVenny,
missionary to Guatemala

It has been said (by who I do not know) that a visionary is someone who can see around the corner and act on it.

"In vision, light is the stimulus input. Light energy goes into the eyes stimulate photoreceptor in eyes. However, as an energy wave, energy is passed on through light at different wavelength. Light as waves carry energy, contains energy by different wavelength."

~Chemistry LibreTexts

To be a true visionary, you must *walk in the light* even when it is dark.

"Practice visioneering and imagineering."

~Rodfucious
from studies by Bob Proctor and Sandy Gallagher

"To be a true visionary you cannot envision your success with logic, which is the desire, dream, vision, imagination, inspiration, thought, idea, goal and plan *killer*."

~Rodfucious

*For you have delivered me from death and my feet from stumbling, that I may walk before God in **the light of life**.*
~Psalm 56:13 emphasis mine

NOTE: There is nothing worse than getting up in the middle of night and stubbing your toe on something. You begin to focus on the pain instead of the purpose for getting up. Sometimes we walk in broad daylight, but our eyes are dark, and we still stumble. As we focus on the negative things in the world and listen to what negative people say, we become blinded and instead of being a visionary, become a "blindonary."

*Blessed are those who have learned to acclaim you, who **walk in the light** of your presence, Lord.*
~Psalm 89:15 emphasis mine

NOTE: When we learn how to acclaim/proclaim God in the dark, we begin to walk in the light, illumination, revelation of His presence. His glory, His presence reveals things to us that we would normally not recognize.

*Come, descendants of Jaco, let us **walk in the light of the Lord**.*
~Isaiah 2:5 emphasis mine

NOTE: Light dwellers are those who have a lineage that is trace back to the Father of lights. Our heritage is light. Because of Jesus we are connected to the light source, and we turn on the light by faith. Remember that "faith without corresponding actions is of none effect." (James 2:17 Weymouth Translation). W activate our faith towards God (Hebrews 6:1) by "walking" out our faith and as we place one foot in front of another, our vision becomes more clear.

We know that Jesus is the light of the world. (John 8:12) But Jesus also said that we (me and you) are the lights of the world. (Matthew 5:14) I believe that part of being a *visionary*, is walking in the light as he is in the light (I John 1:7), and not be hidden (Matthew 5:14), and not let/allow our light to be put under a basket but on a lampstand (Matthew 5:15) as we let/allow our light to shine before men in such a way that they may see your good works and then they can glorify God. (Matthew 5:16)

The people walking in darkness have seen a great light; on those living in the land of deep darkness a light has dawned.
~Isaiah 9:2, Matthew 4:15–16

NOTE: The light is Jesus. I like getting up in the morning when it is still dark. As I am writing this it was dark, but looking out my window, light is piercing the darkness with dawn as the sun rises. Success is like that. We may not be able to see it but when the time is right, an idea my "dawn" on us and as we walk and as the time passes, it progressively gets lighter until we can see clearly.

I am the light of the world. Whoever follows me will never walk in darkness but will have the light of life.
~John 8:12

NOTE: Jesus called people to "follow Me" and that if we did that, they would become fishers of men. (Matthew 4:19) Fishermen, get up early, head out sometimes in the dark and as they fish, the light dawns and they begin to catch fish. I believe that as we follow the light, we can "catch a vision" and become visionaries.

You are going to have the light just a little while longer. Walk while you have the light, before darkness overtakes you. Whoever walks in the dark does not know where they are going. Believe in the light while you have the light, so that you may become children of light.
~John 12:35-36

NOTE: Jesus was speaking of Himself, His Death, Burial, and Resurrection (D.B.R.) and His return to the Father in heaven. The Light was going to be gone, but the light remains in them. Jesus told them, the Light Followers, that they were the lights of the world.

> *You are the light of the world. A city set on a hill cannot be hidden; nor does anyone light a lamp and put it under a basket, but on the lampstand and it give light to all who are in the house. Let your light shine before men in such a way that they may see your good works and glorify your Father who is in heaven.*
>
> ~Matthew 5:14–16

NOTE: Jesus is the Light (Big L) we are the light of the world (little l) and we are to "let our light shine" by the works that we do. I believe that as we have a vision, as we let our dreams, visons and imaginations shine, we are letting our lights shine into a dark world.

> *But if we walk in the light, as he is in the light, we have fellowship with one another, and the blood of Jesus, His Son purifies us from all sin.*
>
> ~I John 1:7

NOTE: The word "fellowship" comes from a Greek word, "koinonia" which means to have something in common, fellowship, communion, community. This connection comes from the light. Where there are people on planet earth, one thing that we have in common is that the sun rises and light pierces the darkness. We have in common the truth that "God so love the world that He gave His only begotten/unique Son (Jesus) that whosoever (open to the current 7.9 + billion people and those how have come and gone before them) believes (trusts in, clings to, relies on, adheres to, cleaves to) Him (Jesus) has everlasting life." (John 3:16) We also have I Thessalonians 5:23 in common, "*Now may the God of peace Himself sanctify you entirely; and may your spirit and soul and body be preserved complete, without blame at the coming of our Lord Jesus Christ.*"

NOTE: If you stand still, you will be in darkness, but if you "walk" in the light, we will "walk in the light of the common day," see clearly, have vision. We will connect with the people that "God so loved."

Where there is no vision, the people perish but he who keepeth the law, happy is he.
~Pro-Verbs 29:18 KJV

Where there is no revelatory vision, the people are unrestrained, but he who keeps the law, happy is he.
~Pro-Verbs 29:18

NOTE: There are multiple translation of this verse. I was told by a missionary in Guatemala that the Spanish translation (from Spanish Bible) speaks of a revelatory vision and people are unrestrained, just doing whatever they want to do. The vision of the Law keeps people in check from their carnal nature.

The thief (religious leaders who allow the traditions of men to nullify the Word of God, the d-evil, false teachers etc.) comes but for to steal (your dreams), kill (your visions) and destroy (your imaginations), but I (Jesus) came to give you (and me) life and that more abundantly (versus mediocrity).
~John 10:10 with emphasis,
additions, and commentary mine, Ruminator Style

NOTE: Not everyone wants you to be prosperous or successful. If they can throw water on the fire of our passionate desires, dreams, visions, imaginations, inspirations, thoughts, ideas, goals and plans, they can bring the darkness back to you and to the world.

The wonderful (full of wonder) thing is that in the darkest night, God has set the stars and the moon with "streams of light into darkened corners" to illuminate our pathways.

In a world of darkness and blindness, in these dark dazes of the pandemic of fear, fueled by systemic sin, manifested with systemic hate, resulting in systemic roots of bitterness around the hearts and minds of the current 8+ billion people of the world, **BE A VISIONARY!**

HOW TO FACE IMPOSSIBILITIES

Have faith in God constantly.
                        ~Mark 11:22, Amplified Bible

And looking at them, Jesus said to them, with people this is impossible, but with God all things are possible.
                        ~Matthew 19:26, Mark 10:27

"If you try to accomplish the impossible with logic, it is impossible to overcome impossibilities."
                        ~Rodfucious

W hen you are working towards success, you will be faced with discouragement and *one of the biggest discouragements is the impossibilities of life.* When you are faced with the obstructions and obstacles of mountains of impossibilities, you will be tempted to *turn around and give up.* Between mountains are shadows which brings on fear and intimidation. I like the saying when we are faced with impossibilities, "But God!" Factor in God, factor in "faith towards God" factor in "belief (trusting in, clinging to, relying on, adhering to, cleaving to) God," factor in "burning desire," factor in "His **SUPER** coming on your natural (also known as His supernatural)," factor in "perseverance" and you have a manifestation of the things desired.

Even though I walk through the valley of the shadow of death I will fear no evil; for Thou art with me.
                        ~Psalm 23:4

Even though I walk through the valley of the shadow of death, I fear no evil and instead of setting up camp in the valley or keep walking around the mountain of the valley, I will keep on walking until I march in the Promised Land and possess what God has promised.

~Psalm 23: 4 with emphasis, additions and commentary mine, Ruminator Style

In Mark 11:22–25 Jesus is teaching His guys (da boys) how to pray the impossible. Previously, before Jesus went back to Jerusalem to cleanse the temple of moneychangers, robbers of the people, Jesus woke up hungry in Bethany. He saw a fig tree that was in leaf in the distance and wondered if possibly there were some figs left on the trees. He went to the fig tree, saw there were no figs and said, *May no one ever eat fruit from you again.* (Mark 11:14) Jesus, the Messiah, the one that his men looked to as their political savior, who was going to deal with the cruelest of governments, the Romans, *was talking to trees.* Of course, He had created the trees so He could talk to the trees. They went on to Jerusalem and He cleansed the temple. (Mark 11:15–18) and then returned to Bethany. They passed by the fig tree that Jesus had been talking to earlier, and they saw that the fig tree was withered from the root up. (Mark 11:20) Peter told Jesus,

Rabbi, look, the fig tree which You cursed (previously spoke to) has withered.

~Mark 11:21 addition mine

Jesus did not try to explain to them what had happened, but merely said, *Have faith in God constantly.* (Mark 11:22 Amplified Bible) Jesus then launched into a teaching how to pray with constant faith in God using mountains as the object of the teaching.

I believe that Jesus was teaching them how to *pray successfully* and how to *get answered prayers* that will lead to their success. One of my favorite authors is Pat Boone. His book *A New Song* deeply affected my spiritual walk which in turned deeply affected my earthly walk.

His book *Pray To Win God Wants You To Succeed* speaks to me now about true Biblical Prosperity and Success.

"Pray to Win explores the greatest source of untapped power in the universe—power that can bring you positive results in every area of your life once you learn how to use it. Through true stories from his own experience and the experience of others, singer-author Pat Boone proves that you can make the miraculous happen in our own life through the power of prayer. Many of the world's busiest and most successful people make this communication with God an integral part of their daily lives because they know that it is an essential ingredient in their success."

~Book jacket from *Pray to Win* by Pat Boone
from the book jacket

*Truly I say to you, whoever **says to this mountain**, be taken up and cast into the sea and does not doubt in his heart but believes that what he says is going to happen, it will be granted him.*
~Mark 11:23

NOTE: The first impossibility was Jesus speaking (cursing) to an inanimate object (a fig tree) and the impossible happens, the tree was withered from the roots up. Now his example of speaking to another inanimate object, a mountain, was within the realm of possibility. Here is how the impossibility of the mountain was faced found in Mark 11:23–25.

1. Speak to the mountain (like a fig tree)
2. Be specific in the speaking (a) be taken up (b) be cast into the sea.
3. Do not doubt that what you spoke will happen
4. Believe (trust in, cling to, rely on, adhere to, cleave to) that what you said is going to happen.
5. It "will be" (not might be, not could be, not if it be God's will) granted him.

THEREFORE: Whenever you see therefore, see what it is there for by referring to previous verse. "Therefore I (Jesus) say to you (those praying with constant faith in God) for which you (a) pray (b) ask (c) believe:"

1. Believe (trust in, cling to, rely on, adhere to, cleave to)
2. That you have (already before you see it manifested) received them
3. It shall be granted you

THE KEY TO SEEING THE IMPOSSIBLITY

This is the key to *seeing the impossibility* in prayer. **Triple AAA Forgiveness:** Whenever you stand praying: (asking for the impossible)

FORGIVE (let it go, leave it loose it)= anything that you are harboring resentment about

1. **A=Anything** (this covers the spectrum of bitterness, resentment, your perceived right to be angry and not forgive)
2. **A=Against** (It does not matter if they have something against you or if they stabbed you in the back)
3. **A=Anyone** (Your spouse, your children, your boss, a corporation, other Christians, political pundits, your church (when they didn't met your every need/greed), yes, even **GOD HIMSELF** because he did not answer you doubting prayers.

So when you have a desire, a dream, a vision, an imagination, an inspiration, a thought, an idea, a goal and a plan, that just seems impossible, don't let that hold you back, tap into the possibility of having he impossible by "having faith in God constantly."

SCOPE OUT THE COMPETITION

...see what the land is like.

~Numbers 13:18

W hile the children of Israel had received from God a promise of land, aka the Promised Land, they still had to go into the land and then possess the land. They could have all the faith in the world but did not put their faith into action by possessing the land, all they would have is an empty promise. Now the empty promise would not be on God, He kept His end of the bargain, but the failure (not success) would be on them.

Then we (Moses and the children of Israel) set out from Horeb and went through all that great and terrible wilderness which you saw on the way to the hill country of the Amorites **JUST AS THE LORD HAD COMMANDED US;** *and we came to Kadesh-Barnea. I (Moses) said to you (the children of Israel), you have come to the hill country of the Amorites which the Lord our God is* **ABOUT TO GIVE US** *(since it was the "promised land"). See (with your own eyes), the Lord your God has* **PLACED THE LAND** *before you; go up and take possession, as thee Lord the God of your fathers, has spoken to you,* **DO NOT FEAR OR BE DISMAYED**.

~Deuteronomy 1:19–21 addition and emphasis mine

I'm convinced that even though they knew God had given them the land, that there would still be an opportunity to *be fearful and overwhelmed* by the inhabitants of the land. Sometimes when you are in a business and you know that God is with you, you still may *tend to be fearful and overwhelmed by your competition.*

COMPETITION: (1) the activity or condition of competing (2) an event or contest in which people compete (3) the person or people with whom one is competing, especially in a commercial or sporting arena, the opposition.

> *Then all of you (the children of Israel) approached me (Moses) and said,* **let us send men before us** *(spies)* **that they may search out the land** *(promised land)* **for us, and bring back to us a word** *(insight)* **of the way by which we should go up and the cities which we shall enter** *(give us a plane).*
>
> Deuteronomy 1:22 addition and emphasis mine

On the surface, it may look like they don't trust God, but I believe that they did trust God, but needed a game plan on *how to enter* and then *possess the land,* **NOT** if they were going in.

> *The thing (the spying) pleased me (Moses) and I took twelve of your men (not just any men, but the cream of the crop, the elite), one man from each tribe. They turned and went up into the hill country and came to the valley of Eschol (grapes) and spied it out.*
>
> ~Deuteronomy 1:23–24

NOTE: This is where the *reconnaissance mission* took a turn for the worse and ten spies gave out a bad report while two gave out a good report. Read Deuteronomy 1:25–46 and Numbers 13:1–33 for further details.

Marketing is key to success of any endeavor.

MARKETING: The activity or business of promoting and selling products or services, including market research and advertising.

I believe that one of the main components of marketing, the R.A.M., the Results, Achievements, Manifestation of any endeavor including your personal, relational, spiritual, and financial life. I teach that we all have the God given potential to reach or R.A.M. in our desires, dreams, visions, imaginations, inspirations, thoughts, ideas, and plans. Recently, I have been ruminating on the process and came up with these ideas.

HOW TO WORK OUT THE RESULTS, ACHIEVMENTS, MANIFESATIONS OF ANYTHING IN OUR LIVES.

I am a big believer in taking our desires, dreams, visions, imaginations, inspirations, thoughts, ideas, goals, and plans **AND** accomplishing our *R.A.M.=Results, Achievements, Manifestations.* The problem arises when we don't accomplish our *R.A.M.* and we give up not only of our *R.A.M.*, but also on ever trying anything again. We end up in a heap of condemnation and shame and then we just settle for "Que, Sera, Sera."

We begin to think failure, speak failure and act like we are a failure and thus, we become failures. The problem is when we *DON'T SEE* or *EXPERIENCE* our desired results, our expected achievements, our expected manifestations.

As I am ruminating on this, the thought came into my mind that we tend to work the *wrong way.* We tend to work from *NOTHING* (working from scratch) with only our desires, visions, imaginations, inspirations, thoughts, ideas, goals, and plans and struggle forward towards the *R.A.M.* and then we try to work forward (many times with no insights). Now, it is not wrong to having what we want to work toward, but we must live/walk by faith and *NOT* by sight.

When we don't *SEE* our results, achievements, manifestations, *ONLY SEE* our failures and we tend to *GIVE UP!* The Word of God (the Bible, the Manufacturer's Handbook, the Communication Manuel) tells us how to *LIVE* and *WALK.*

Now, faith is the substance of things hoped for, the evidence of things not seen.

~Hebrews 11:1

Now faith is the assurance (substance, the confirmations, the title deed) of the things (desires, visions, imaginations, inspirations, thoughts, ideas, goals, and plans) Rodney Lewis Boyd (put your name here) hopes for (confidently expects), being the proof (evidence) of things (desires, dreams, visions, imaginations, inspirations, thoughts, ideas, goals, and plans) Rodney Lewis Boyd DO NOT SEE (revealed to the senses including sight, sound, smell, taste, touch) and the conviction (where we know that we know that we know) of their (things,=the desires, dreams, visions, imaginations, inspirations, thoughts, ideas, goals, and plans) REALITY (faith perceiving (observing, seeing) sensing, as real fact what is NOT REVEALED to the senses (including sight, sound, smell, taste, touch)].

~Hebrews 11:1 with emphasis,
additions, commentary mine, Ruminator Style

"The righteous (2 Corinthians 5:17,21) shall live by faith."
~Romans 1:17, Habakkuk 2:4, Galatians 3:11,
Hebrews 10:38 addition mine

For in the Gospel (the Death, Burial, Resurrection, the D.B.R.) a righteousness which god ascribes which God ascribes is REVEALED (a revelatory vision), both springing from FAITH and leading to FAITH [disclosed through the way of FAITH that arouses to more FAITH . As it is written, the man thought FAITH is just and upright shall LIVE and shall LIVE BY FAITH.

~Romans 1:17, Habakkuk 2:4, Galatians 3:11,
Hebrews 10:38 additions and emphasis mine

For we walk by faith and not by sight.
~2 Corinthians 5:7

For we (Rodney Lewis Boyd and you)WALK BY FAITH [we regulate our lives and conduct ourselves by our conviction or belief respecting man's relationship to god and divine things, with trust and holy fervor; thus we WALK] not by sight (what we see) or

appearance (how things look from the external with the senses like, sight, sound, smell, taste, touch).
~2 Corinthians 5:7, Amplified Bible with emphasis, addition, commentary, mine, Ruminator Style

I believe, and am coming into an understanding, that we should *work backwards*, where we come from the *R.A.M.* (what we want) and then work backwards *AS* God gives us the various steps to take towards the *R.A.M.* in our lives and then begin to apply the practical steps need to move towards the *R.A.M.* This takes *FAITH*. To the mind, this is illogical. Logic is the dream killer; logic walks by SIGHT and not by FAITH.

"The thief comes only to steal and kill and destroy; I came that they might have life and might have it abundantly."
~John 10:10

The thief comes only in order to steal and kill and destroy. I came that they may have life, and have it in abundance (to the full, till it overflows).
~John 10:10 Amplified Bible

The thief (corrupt religious leaders, the d-evil) comes (and they will come) in order to (the reason they come) to steal your dreams, to kill your visions and to destroy your imaginations, BUT (in contrast) I (Jesus) came that you may have life (not death by mediocrity) and have this life in abundance (to the full until it overflows).
~John 10:10 with emphasis, additions, and commentary mine, Ruminator Style)

Jesus, the One who came to give us an abundant life (verses the mediocre life) tells us how to "have faith in God constantly) and how to speak to obstructions, obstacles, mountains of impossibilities, and the keys to prayer and accomplishing R.A.M. (Mark 11:22–26)

Have faith in God (not your desires, dreams, visions, imagination,

inspirations, thoughts, ideas, goals, and plans) CONSTANTLY.
~Mark 11:22 Amplified Bible with emphasis,
additions, and commentary mine.

This is what Jesus told his followers to do when they saw the results of a fig tree being withered from the roots up after He spoke to the fig tree. (Mark 11:13, Mark 11:20–21, Mark 11:22)

Jesus launched into a teaching about how to pray impossible prayers.

MARK 11:22-25

1. Have faith in God and not what you see.
2. Speak to the mountain (the impossibility standing in your way)
3. Be specific in speaking what you want, not what you've got.
4. When you speak do not doubt in your heart.
5. When you speak, believe (trust in, cling to , rely on, adhere to, cleave to)
6. Believe that what you say, "is "*GOING to happen,*" even when you don't see it happening.
7. Pray, Ask, Believe that you *HAVE RECEIVED THEM* ,and they *SHALL BE GRANTED* you.
8. Practice Triple AAA forgiveness—A=Anything A=Against, A=Anyone (matters not what they have done to you)

A=Against (whatever you are holding against someone)
A=Anyone (whosoever has done you wrong

When you apply constant faith in God in your prayers, you are not praying to get, but thanking God for what you have already, working from R.A.M. backwards. That's my story and I'm sticking to it.

In whatever endeavor that you are doing, it is good to *enter in with your eyes wide open*, and *scope out the territory and competition,* but *keep in mind that the victory is yours,* especially when you know that you, "can do all things through Christ Who strengthens you" (Philippians 4:3 and that your "God shall supply all your needs according to His riches in glory in Christ Jesus." Philippians 4:19

THE BUSINESS OF A GOD (GOOD) REPORT

When they returned from spying out the land, at the end of forty days, they proceeded to come to Moses and Aaron and to all the congregation of the sons of Israel in the wilderness of Param, at Kadesh: and they brought back word to them and to all the congregation and showed them the fruit of the land.

~Numbers 13:25–26

In our **SECRETS TO SUCCESS # 23** we saw the power of a report. One was a **BAD REPORT** (a d-evil report) and the other was a **GOOD REPORT** (a God report).

The bad report was based on fear and spoke of what the could NOT do while the good report was based on what they could and should do.

Thus they (the 12 spies) to him (Moses) and said, went in to the land where you sent us (at their request, Deuteronomy 1:22-24) and it certainly does flow with milk and honey, and this is its fruit (so far so good).

~Numbers 13:27 additions mine

NEVERTHELESS *(in spite of the goodness of the land), the people who live in the land are strong and the cities are fortified and very large; and* **MOREOVER**, *(and in addition to that) we SAW (walking by sight and not by faith) the descendants of Anak there. Amalk is living in the land of the Negev and the Hittites and the Jebusites, and the Amorites are living in the hill country and*

the Canaanites (and all of the other-ites) are living by the side of the sea and by the side of the Jordan.
~Numbers 13:28–29 additions and emphasis mine

The bad report had two words that were faith negaters:
1. Nevertheless
2. Moreover

These words can negate your success in the business world. That does not mean that you deny the negative, but you don't allow the negative to influence your next move.

Then Caleb (along with Joshua) quieted the people (negativity insights negativity), before Moses and said We should by all means (1) go up and take possession of it (2) for we shall overcome it.
~Numbers 13:30 additions mine

And so everyone changed their minds and did not let the bad report affect them. **NOT!**

But the men who had gone up with him said, we **ARE NOT ABLE** *to go up against the people, for they are* **TOO STRONG FOR US.**
~Numbers 13:31 emphasis mine

When you are faced with the *giants in the business world*, we are not able to go up against the competition or the odds against us, for the competition is **TOO STRONG FOR US.** So we give up and just let our desires, visons, goals, imaginations, inspirations, thoughts, ideas, goals and plans blow away like a feather in a hurricane. In the movie *The Shawshank Redemption*, when the warden discovered that Andy Dufresne had escaped from institutional bondage, he declared, "A man up and vanished like a fart in the wind." That gives a whole new meaning to "the smell of fear."

So they gave out to the sons of Israel **A BAD** *(negative)* **REPORT** *of the land (that God had promised them), which they*

had spied out, saying the land through which we have gone in spying it out is a land that devours its inhabitants; and all the people whom we saw in it are of great size (the competition is too big).
~Numbers 13:32 additions and emphasis mine

There never was a denial of the validity of what they were reporting, only a difference in the outcomes.

There also we saw the Nephilim (the sons of Anak) are part of the Nephilim; and we **BECAME** *(went from one state to another) like grasshoppers (very small)* **IN OUR OWN SIGHT**.
~Numbers 13:33 additions and emphasis mine

How we see ourselves compared to others, especially our competition, is how **THEY WILL SEE US** and show us no mercy. The *secret to success is our self-esteem*, how we see ourselves.

The enemy, the competition, the d-evil can smell the fear on us. A bad report stinks and a good report can be a pleasing aroma. It all depends on the person sniffing around you.

But thanks be to God, who always leads us in His triumph in Christ, and manifests through us **the sweet aroma** *of the knowledge of Him in every place. For we are* **a fragrance** *of Christ to God among those who are being saved and those who are perishing; to one* **an aroma from death to death**, *to the other and* **aroma from life to life**. *And who is adequate for these things? For we are not like may, peddling the Word of God, but a from sincerity, but as from God, we speak in Christ in the sight of God.*
2 Corinthians 2:14–17 emphasis mine

I am convinced that what we think, speak and do determine how others smell us. Changing the way that you think, speak and do (a Paradigm Shift/Mindset Change) will change the outcome, change the Results, Achievements, Manifestations in our life and our business. Some would say, "mind your own business," I say, "mind God's business and your own business will take care of itself."

I was recently riding down the road as Brenda was driving and as usual, I had my trusty steno pad, writing down random thoughts. Who knew I would be typing them into this section of the book.

- "Quit speaking what you've got but speak what you want."
- "Start speaking your desires, dreams, visions, imaginations, inspirations, thoughts, ideas, plans and goals."
- "Quit thinking, speaking and acting negatively."
- "Start thinking, speaking and acting positively."
- "What comes out of your mouth (aka your piehole) when you are shaken by the external forces in the world, reveals your internal and determines your outcomes."
- "We must call our desires, dreams, visions, imaginations, inspirations, thoughts, ideas, goals and plans that **ARE NOT** as thought **THEY WERE** instead of calling our desires, dreams, visions, imaginations, inspirations, thoughts ideas, goals and plans **AS IF THEY WILL NEVER HAPPEN."**
- "We limit our own future by our own logic."
- "Logic may seem practical (dare I say logical) but logic is the desire, dream, vision, imagination, inspiration, thought, idea, goals and plans **KILLER!"**

NOTE: When Emerson Grace, How Sweet the Sound saw me write something on my pad, she said, Gaggy (G-AH-GE) "are you writing a book?" I told her that I was just writing stuff that I thought about, but it may turn into a book. Now, here it is, in the book. In a misquote of the words of Hannibal Smith on the television show The A-Team, "I love it when a desire, dream, vision, imagination, inspiration, thought, idea, goal and plan comes together."

THE POWER OF PARADIGMS/MINDSETS

POWER/AUTHORITY: exousia (*ex-oo-see'-ah)*=From G1832 (in the sense of *ability*); *privilege*, that is, (subjectively) *force*, *capacity*, *competency*, *freedom*, or (objectively) *mastery* (concretely *magistrate*, *superhuman*, *potentate*, *token of control*), delegated *influence:* - authority, jurisdiction, liberty, power, right, strength. **G1832: exesti (*ex'-es-tee)=*** impersonally *it is right* (through the figurative idea of *being out* in public): - be lawful, let, X may (-est).

> *For the mind set on the flesh is death, but the mind set on the Spirit is life and peace.\"*
>
> ~Romans 8:6

POWER/ABILITY: Dunamis (*doo'-nam-is)=*From G1410; *force* (literally or figuratively); specifically miraculous *power* (usually by implication a *miracle* itself): - ability, abundance, meaning, might (-ily, -y, -y deed), (worker of) miracle (-s), power, strength, violence, mighty (wonderful) work. **G1410: dunamis (*doo'-nam-is)=*From** G1410; *force* (literally or figuratively); specifically miraculous *power* (usually by implication a *miracle* itself): - ability, abundance, meaning, might (-ily, -y, -y deed), (worker of) miracle (-s), power, strength, violence, mighty (wonderful) work.

PARADIGM: (1) a mental program that has almost exclusive control over our habitual behavior, and almost all of our behavior is habitual (2) a mental program that is developed by (a) nature, from D.N.A. strands from the Garden of Eden (b) nurture, environmental influences from birth until there is a shift in our thinking.

MINDSET: (1) The Mind Set is a verb of what our mind is set/focused on (good, bad, ugly) that will become a noun called MINDSET, the collective thinking that determines our R.A.M.=results, achievements, manifestations in our lives (good, bad, ugly).

The mindset is what your mind is habitually set on. If your mind is habitually set on the flesh, the carnal nature, the things against God, the d-evil, the cause and effect is death. Your mind set on the flesh will take you to a lifeless, mediocre life. This mindset is aka your paradigm, a mental program (from pre-birth to birth and then after birth the process continues to form what you habitually think, speak and do bringing you the results in your life and almost all of our ways are habitually.

If you are constantly thinking, speaking, and doing what you can't do, you never will do it.

You must have a Paradigm Shift, a change in Mindset. This can only take place by your free will, your choice to think on the positive things of life.

This thing called Paradigm/Mindset originally started in the Garden of Eden when Adam and Eve chose to disobey God thus committing high treason. The cause and effect of their choice was passed down from generation to generation with its negative effects. Once you were born, if there is negativity around you that will also form a negative paradigm/mindset.

One of the ways that you can tell IF you need a Paradigm Shift/ Mindset change is your soul. The soul (psuche/psych) is made up of your mind (what you think) your volition (what you freely choose based on what you think) and your emotions (the barometer of your emotions).

Emotions includes confusion, sad, strong happy, anger, energized and multiple others that affects our lives. The soul (psuche/psych) includes our minds (what we habitually think about) our will (our volition, free will, what we choose based on what we think) and our emotions (the barometer of our feelings) According to englishstudy-here.com emotions includes (but is not limited to):

CONFUSION
Uncertain
Upset
Doubtful
Uncertain
Indecisive
Perplexed
Embarrassed
Hesitant
Shy
Lost
Unsure
Pessimistic
Tense

"For God is NOT a God of confusion but of peace, as in all the churches of the saints."

~1 Corinthians 14:33 emphasis mine

Why would I keep all of these characteristics of confusion in my life and allowing them to dictate my life? When these things appear, they are indicators that I need to shift my paradigm and change the way that I am thinking, speaking, and doing things that will lead to success. Take some time and write the antonym of each of these confusing characteristics, for example, uncertain/certainty, upset/at ease, doubtful/confident, decisive, certain. Instead of being confused, uncertain, upset and doubtful, begin to think certainty, at ease, confident, decisive, certain and then begin to speak and act like what you want.

SAD
Depressed
Desperate
Dejected
Heavy
Crushed

Disgusted
Upset
Hateful
Sorrowful
Mournful
Weepy
Frustrated

Now, when you are sad, begin to think, speak and act the opposite like depressed/cheerful, desperate/composed, dejected/happy/cheerful, heavy/light, frustrated/satisfaction. You get the idea. If you are frustrated and you have renewed your mind with The Rollings Stones song, "I can't get no satisfaction," counter that with yes I can!

ANGER

Annoyed
Agitated
Fed up
Irritated
Mad
Critical
Resentful
Disgusted
Outraged
Raging
Furious
Livid
Bitter

If you are angry, you can take authority of that emotion and shift and change it. Like Brenda's mom use to tell her when Brenda would say, "I'M MAD," "You can get glad just as quick as you got mad." So can you. When Cain was angry with God and his brother Able, God came down and put his finger on the problem.

...so Cain became **VERY ANGRY** *and his countenance (how his*

face looked, reflecting his emotion) fell. Then the Lord said to Cain why are you angry? And why has your countenance fallen? If you do well (your choice) will not your countenance be lifted up? And if you do not do well (his choice), sin is crouching at your door (if you are angry in the flesh you are sinning) ; and its (sin and anger) desire is for you, **BUT YOU MUST MASTER IT.**

~Genesis 4:3–7 emphasis and additions mine

Now, find the antonym for the gamut of anger emotions, including annoyed/pleased, agitated/calm, and relaxed, irritated/contented/ good humor, livid/brilliant/cheerful/happy/radiant.

These are just a few examples of a Paradigm Shift/Mind Change. You must (it ain't an option) renew you mind with the Word of God.

Rejoice in the Lord always and again I say rejoice.

~Philippians 4:4)

Rejoice always.

~I Thessalonians 5:16

In everything (good, bad, ugly) give thanks, this is the will of God (the giving of thanks) for you in Christ Jesus.

~I Thessalonians 5:18 additions mine

The steadfast of mind, Thou will keep in perfect peace because it is stayed on you.

~Isaiah 26:30

The Spirit of the Lord God is upon me (the anointing), because the Lord has anointed Me (Jesus teaching, Luke 4:18) to bring the good (not bad) news to the afflicted; He has sent me to bind up the brokenhearted, to proclaim liberty to captives, and freedom to prisoners; to proclaim the favorable year of the Lord, and the day of vengeance of our God; to comfort all who mourn in Zion, giving them a garland instead of ashes, the oil of gladness instead of mourning, the mantle of praise instead of a spirit of fainting. So they will be called oaks of righteousness, the planting of the Lord that He may be glorified.

~Isaiah 61:1–3

I like to continue with reading about the cause and effect of Isaiah 61:1-3) found in Isaiah 61:4–7:

- Then they will rebuild the ancient ruins
- They will raise up the former devastations
- They will repair the ruined cities
- Strangers will stand and pasture your flocks
- Foreigners will be your farmers and you vinedressers
- You will be called the priests of the Lord
- You will be spoke of as ministers of God
- You will eat the wealth of the nations
- In their riches you will boast
- Instead of shame you will have a double portion
- Instead of humiliation they will shout for joy over their portion
- They will posses a double portion in their land
- Everlasting joy will be theirs.

WOW! Let me say that backwards **WOW! OR** you could just languish in your emotional meltdown. It is like choosing between a curse and a blessing, life, and death.

I call heaven and earth to witness against you today, that I have set before you life and death, the blessing, and the curse, (confusion/clarity, depression/joy, anger/calmness, etc.). So choose life in order that you may live, you and your descendants."

~Deuteronomy 30:19 additions mine

What you choose will determine your success.

Depending on what your *emotion* is will determine **IF** or **IF NOT,** you need to have a Paradigm Shift in your life. You merely begin to focus on the positive and reject the negative. Usually, you need to also have an **ATTITUDINAL ADJUSTMENT.**

*Have **this attitude** in yourselves, which was also **in Christ Jesus,** who although He existed in the form of God, did not regard equality with God a thing to be grasped, but emptied Himself, taking the form of a bond-servant and being made in the likeness of men.*
~Philippians 2:5–7 emphasis mine

Part of the Paradigm Shift/Mindset Change you must *be emptied* of your human attitude and replace them with *God tendencies.* This means *getting on God's frequency and vibrations* and off of your *emotional negative frequency and vibrations.*

I am convinced that everything has a frequency and vibration and if your frequency and vibration is set on negativity, so will your emotions be negative and visa-versa. Frequencies and vibrations are found in everything from solid rock to water, from thought waves to solid wood, to the miracle of our vocal folds vibrating at a certain frequency to our ears who receive the voice frequency and vibration to our connectivity to the Creator to the universe to the universe itself.

We always seem to come around to these Scriptures verses when talking about Paradigms/Mindsets.

*As a man **THINKS** in his heart/mind **SO** he is.*
Pro-Verbs 23:7

...out of the abundance (overflow) of the heart/mind **THE MOUTH SPEAKS**.
~Luke 6:45 addition and emphasis mine

FAITH *(what you believe) without* **CORRESPONDING ACTIONS** *(works) is of none effect (dead).*
~James 2:17 The Weymouth Translation with emphasis, additions, commentary mine, Ruminator Style

The **MIND SET** *(focused on what hat develops your* **MIND-SET***) on the flesh (the negative carnal nature) is death (lifeless mediocrity)* **BUT** *(in contrast to) the* **MIND SET** *(focused on what hat develops your* **MINDSET***) on the Spirit (the positive* *spiritual nature) is life (full of vibrance and abundance) is life (and that more abundant) and peace (wholeness and rest).*

~Romans 8:6 with additions,
emphasis, and commentary mine, Ruminator Style

IF you don't keep your Paradigm/Mindset set on the positive then you will default to the negative and in essence derail any hope of **SUCCESS**, and now you know the **SECRET.**

LIVE ABUNDANTLY

The thief comes only to steal and kill and destroy, I came that they may have life, and have it (more) abundantly.
                                              ~John 10:10, addition mine

MORE ABUNDANTLY: perissos (*per-is-sos'*)=From G4012 (in the sense of *beyond*); *superabundant* (in quantity) or *superior* (in quality); by implication *excessive*; adverb (with G1537) *violently*; neuter (as noun) *preeminence:* - exceeding abundantly above, more abundantly, advantage, exceedingly, very highly, beyond measure, more, superfluous, vehement [-ly]. **G4012: peri (*per-ee'*)**=From the base of G4008; properly *through* (all *over*), that is, *around*; figuratively *with respect* to; used in various applications, of place, cause or time (with the genitive case denoting the *subject* or *occasion* or *superlative* point; with the accusative case the *locality, circuit, matter, circumstance* or general *period*): - (there-) about, above, against, at, on behalf of, X and his company, which concern, (as) concerning, for, X how it will go with, ([there-, where-]) of, on, over, pertaining (to), for sake, X (e-) state, (as) touching, [where-] by (in), with. In compounds it retains substantially the same meaning of circuit (*around*), excess (*beyond*), or completeness (*through*). **G4008: peran (*per'-an*)**=Apparently the accusative case of an obsolete derivation of πείρω peirō (to "peirce"); *through* (as adverb or preposition), that is, *across:* - beyond, farther (other) side, over.

True success is not a lack and not just abundance, but it is more abundantly, overflowing, over the top.

There is a thief who is trying to keep you from an abundant life and wanting you to be a failure and not successful. Jesus is talking about a thief, corrupt, false religious teachers). These thieves come to steal (what is yours) kill (you) and destroy (pull you down) BUT (in contrast to the thief) I (Jesus) came that you might have life (instead of death) and that more abundantly (overflowing)." (John 10:10 with emphasis and additions and commentary mind, Ruminator Style) In your everyday life, the thief (competition) comes to steal (rob you of what is yours) kill (your desires) and destroy (your success).

The thief (the d-evil, religion, your competitor) comes to kill your dreams, steal your visions and destroy your imaginations, inspirations, thoughts ideas, goals and plans, so that you will have an impoverished and mediocre life, but Jesus came to give your life and not just life but a more abundant life.
~John 10:10 with emphasis, additions,
and commentary mine, Ruminator Style

Beloved, I wish above (abundantly above) all things that you might prosper, be in health, even as your soul prospers."
~3 John 2 addition mine

IF you have a choice (and you do) choose abundant life versus choosing to allow the thief to kill, steal and destroy and give you a mediocre life.

The **PARADIGM/MINDSET** is not located in the brain (part of the body) but in the soul (the mind, volition, emotions). The brain is the complex neurological switching station that sends the electrical impulses to various parts of the body that controls what we do. Now, there most likely is a connection between soul (mind) and body (brain/nerves), but I believe (I think I'm right, but I could be wrong) that the primary part of the mind is in the soul. The mind set is a verb that when implemented becomes the noun of the mindset/paradigm.

PARADIGM/MINDSET DEVELOPEMNT/CORRUPTED/RESTORED

The *paradigm and mindset* is developed from "in the beginning" until now on the time-space continuum.

- The original *paradigm/mindset* was when God created man/woman with the free will (volition) to choose. (Genesis 1:26–27, Genesis 2:7, Genesis 2:7, Genesis 2:20–25) God's view of the creation of man and womankind was that, "And God saw all that He had made, and behold, it was very good... (including the *paradigm/mindset*)." (Genesis 1:31)

- The *paradigm/mindset* was corrupted when the man/woman choose freely to violate the commandment of God and chose to do what they wanted to do. (Genesis 2: 16–17) With their choose came consequences to their actions, the cause and effect of choice which was sin/the curse/death/dying/and a skewed mindset where, "wickedness of man was great in the earth, and that every thought/imagination/imagining was only evil continually." (Genesis 6:5) This corruption was passed down from generation to generation where, "just as through one man (Adam and Eve) sin entered into the world and death through sin, and so death spread to all men (mankind) for all sinned." (Romans 5:12) This was the beginning of a negative **paradigm/mindset** *and* all that is *negative* on Planet Earth. This skewed spiritual D.N.A. contaminated the mental and physical D.N.A. as it is passed down from A & E through time to your mom and dad and after they came together sexually (the knew each each other) and nine months later BAM... to you. This is when your initial *paradigm* and mindset was developed, called *nature*. Every negative event from murder, war,deformity, etc. was set into motion.

- **PHASE 2** of the *paradigm/mindset* development takes place by what is known as nurture/environmental including your familial surroundings,school, friends, your friends parents, social media, television/radio, music/movies, etc. We soak in information (good, bad, ugly) and process the information through the *paradigm* and *mindset* which in turn influences our lives. There must be a shift/change in how we think, speak, and act if we want different *R.A.M.*, results, achievements, manifestations. As every thought of man is evil which in turn opens the door for every action of man to be evil and man and womankind begins to "...call evil good and good evil...and substitute darkness for light and light for darkness...and substitute bitter for sweet and sweet for bitter" and habitually sin.

- The shift/change of the skewed/corrupt paradigm/mindset must be on the spiritual level because it was lost on the spiritual level. I believe that the start is being born again/born anew/born from above. There must be a new and fresh start that comes from becoming a **NEW CREATION** where the **OLD THINGS** passed away and **NEW** and **FRESH THINGS** are constantly coming (2 Corinthians 5:17, 21) Even with all of the new changes in the spiritual changes there is still the old thoughts that come alive and try to bring you back down which leads to the next phase of change.

- The *paradigm shift/mindset change* must be implemented daily. What you think, what you say, and what you do must be done on purpose for a purpose. Many of the epistles (letters) in the New Testament are written to believers who have fallen back into their old *paradigm/mindsets*.

It was for freedom that Christ set us free (we really were set free); therefore keep standing firm and do not be subject again to a yoke of slavery."
~Galatians 5:1 addition mine

"The *mind set* on the flesh is death, but the *mind set* on the Spirit is life and peace.
~Romans 8:6 emphasis mine

As a man/woman *thinks* in their hearts/minds *so they are."*
~Pro-Verbs 23:7 addition and emphasis mine

"...out of the abundance of the heart/mind *the mouth speaks."*
~Luke 6:45 emphasis mine

*Faith without **corresponding actions** is of none effect."*
~James 2:16 emphasis mine

And do not be ***conformed*** to this world, but be ***transformed*** by ***the renewing of your mind***, that you may prove what the will of God is, that which is good, acceptable, and perfect.
~Romans 12:2 emphasis mine

*Put off your **old self**, which belongs to your former manner of life and is corrupt through deceitful desires, and to **be renewed in the spirit of your minds**, and to **put on the new self**, created in the likeness of God in true righteousness and holiness.*
~Ephesians 4:22–24

Casting down imaginations, *and every high thing that exalts itself against the knowledge of God and bringing into captivity every thought to the obedience of Christ.*
~2 Corinthians 10:5 emphasis

So, what does all of this have to do with success? Everything! What you *think* (your paradigm and mindset) and what you *say* (expressing what you think) and what you *do* (how you act based on what you think and say) will determine the R.A.M., the results, achievements and manifestations of your success or failure. We must learn how to shift our paradigms and change our mindsets to shift and change our actions.

When I ask people to choose, I think of the beer commercial where the most interesting man in the world starts off with, "I don't always…" In my mind I hear, "I don't always choose to be prosperous and successful…oh wait, yes I do."

THE WALK AND LIFESTYLE OF FAITH

> *Walk by faith and not by sight.*
>   ~2 Corinthians 5:7 emphasis mine

WALK: peripateō (*per-ee-pat-eh'-o*)= to *tread* all *around*, that is, *walk* at large (especially as proof of ability); figuratively to *live, deport oneself, follow* (as a companion or votary): - go, be occupied with, walk (about).

> *The righteous **shall live by faith**.*
>   Romans 1:17, Habakkuk 2:4, Galatians 3:1,
>   Hebrews 10:38 emphasis mine

LIVE: zaō (*dzah'-o*)= A primary verb; to *live* (literally or figuratively): - life (-time), (a-) live (-ly), quick.

Walking and living is not a job where you clock in and out. Walking and living is not like a vampire movie where you climb back into your coffin at the first sign of daylight and then come out at night. Walking and living is not like a zombie thriller where the walking dead appears at night, like cockroaches, and dry to get you to come over to their side. No, in the natural, walking and living is a 7/24/365 living and breathing lifestyle. Success is not a nine to five job, success is a 7/24/365 opportunity to be who you are, a success. The saying is Carpe Diem, *seize the day!*

If you don't keep walking, keep exercising your muscles, your muscles will atrophy (weaken) and you will no longer be walking. If you don't keep breathing, you are dead.

"The opportunity of a lifetime must be seized in the lifetime of the opportunity."

~Leonard Ravenhill

"Faith sees the opportunity and seizes it."

~Rodfucious

Now faith is the substance of things hoped for, the evidence of things not seen.

~Hebrews 11:1

HOPED: elpizō (*el-pid'-zo)*=From G1680; to *expect* or *confide:* - (have, thing) hope (-d) (for), tru **G1680: elpis (*el-pece')*=**From ἔλπω elpō which is a primary word (to *anticipate*, usually with pleasure); *expectation* (abstract or concrete) or *confidence:* - faith, hope.

Now faith is the assurance (the confirmation, the title deed) of the things [we] hope for, being the proof of things [we] do not see and the conviction of their reality [faith perceiving as real fact what is not revealed to the senses].

~Hebrews 11:1 Amplified Bible

For true success to come, faith must be initiated, walked, and lived out 7/24/365. Now, don't get me wrong, a human being can do powerful things as they pull up their own bootstraps, and through tenacity and the indomitable spirit can accomplish anything that they set their minds to, but in the end, true prosperity and success will be reflected in whom they give credit.

Have faith in God constantly.

~Mark 11:22 Amplified Bible

You can have faith in anyone and anything and you can be consistent in your faith, but your faith is only as good as who and what you place your faith in. You can have faith in your desires, dreams, visions, imaginations, inspirations, thoughts, ideas, goals and plans and still come up short, when your walk and lifestyle fall apart and fail. You see them fall apart and fail, because your sight and faith is in the wrong things.

Your faith must be directional, towards God (Hebrews 6:1) and God's power is directional, towards you (Ephesians 1:19). When your faith is towards God and His power is toward those who believe, that is where His **SUPER** comes on our natural and God stuff happens in our lives.

I truly believe that true prosperity and success, in how passionate you believe in your services and how you begin to serve others, and help others rise to the top.

> *Now (faith is in the now) faith (what you believe in, trust in, cling to, rely on, adhere to, cleave to) is the substance (tangible energy) of things (a person, place or thing) hoped for (confidently expected) the evidence (hard, cold, stone facts and proof) of things (a person, place or thing)* **NOT SEEN** *(or revealed to the senses including sight, sound, smell, taste and touch).*
> ~Hebrews 11:1 with emphasis, additions, and commentary mine, Ruminator Style)

Back in the day, I practiced the martial arts, the art of karate (the art of the empty hand). I started when I was 21 and then quit, but when I turned 48 I started telling whoever would listen to me, from my wife, my son, my dog, that when I turned 50 years old that I would start karate again and get my Black Belt. I did not have a Black Belt, but I had a burning desire, vision, imagination, inspiration, thought, idea, goals, and plan, that I would get my Black Belt.

After years and years and years, and then more years of practice, sweat, setbacks, I became a Black Belt and proceeded to get my 2nd degree Black Belt (after more years of practice, sweat, setbacks). After a (not my, I don't claim it) stroke in 2017 (aka setback) in my mind I still see me getting my 3rd degree Black Belt). I have pictures (physical and mental) of when the first Black Belt was wrapped around my waist. This was a sign of success.

I eventually was blessed and honored to be able to teach karate to beginners (who earned a white belt, the first of many belts including their gold, blue, orange, green, purple, brown then black). One thing that I taught them was that before you could obtain a Black Belt around their waist, the must have a Black Belt in their mind. This is an act of faith that they must live, walk, and act it out by faith. So it is with any area of success in your life.

Just like life, before you experience success, you must first, by faith have it in your mind.

LEARN THE ART OF ANXIETY BUSTING

*Be anxious for nothing, but in everything by prayer and suppli-
cation with thanksgiving, let your request be made known to God.*
~Philippians 4:6

ANXIOUS/ANXIETY: merimnaō (*mer-im-nah'-o)***=**From G3308;
to *be anxious* about: - (be, have) care (-ful), take thought. G3308:
merimna (*mer'-im-nah)*=From G3307 (through the idea of *distraction)*; *solicitude:* - care. G3307: merizō (*mer-id'-zo)*=From G3313; to
part, that is, (literally) to *apportion,* bestow, share, or (figuratively) to
disunite, differ: - deal, be difference between, distribute, divide, give
part. G3313: meros (*mer'-os)*=From an obsolete but more primary
form of μείρομαι meiromai (to *get* as a *section* or *allotment)*; a *division*
or *share* (literally or figuratively, in a wide application): - behalf, coast,
course, craft, particular (+ -ly), part (+ -ly), piece, portion, respect,
side, some sort (-what). (Strong's Concordance of Old and New
Testament Definitions)

SOLICIDTUDE: (1) the state of being concerned and anxious (2)
a cause of care or concern (Merriam-Webster Dictionary)

ANXIETY: Being mentally pulled in twenty different directions
being unable to focus on anything. (The Ruminator Definition of
Word Meanings)

Solicitude/overly caring about something or someone is a bad
thing. I'm not talking about the care of a mother for her children,

or the care of a nurse who has compassion for her patients, or the care for life in general, but when that care, that solicitude, turns into toxic anxiety and worry, I draw the line. Now, if someone says to me, "take care" my default in my minds is, "No thank you, I don't think so." If someone tells me to drive "carefully," my default in my mind is, "No, but I will drive "prayerfully."

As you set out on your adventure of success, you can't have a paradigm/*mindset of anxiety.*

When you are setting out to be a success, most likely you will be distracted by anxiety, worry, tension, doubt, fear, unbelief that will keep you from keeping your eye on the prize and accomplishing success. These distractions can be anything from political upheaval, fluctuating Wall Street bull and bear markets, rising and falling gas prices, negative world events, anything that makes you focus on anything other than success. IF your mind is constantly on the bottom line, then you will be distracted from the reason you got in the business in the first place.

Anxiety (and its second cousin, logic) will make you think (obsess) that you do not need to let/allow God to know what your request is. Anxiety will make you think (obsess) that you have to accomplish success on your own, so you just pull up your own bootstraps and still fail miserably. Anxiety will make you think (obsess) that you do not have to resist the d-evil and then you will allow the d-evil to devour you.

QUESTIONS

- What are we not to let/allow to enter into our lives? (Philippians 4:6)
- But in contrast what are we to pray about? (Philippians 4:6)

NOTE: Take a sheet of paper and draw a line down the middle. At the top of the page on one side, write **NOTHING** and on the other side write **EVERYTHING**. Now, on the nothing side, write down all the things that you are anxious about, and then draw an arrow from the nothing side to the everything side. Why? Because there are the exact same things. Now begin to talk to God about them and start supplicating (being humbly specific). Don't just pray, "Lord I need money. Be specific about what you need the money. Lord, I need $182.68 for my electric bill. Now start thinking him for providing the $182.68 **BEFORE** you ever see it.

- What three thing do you need to do about what is causing the anxiety? (Philippians 4:6)

1.

2.

3.

PRAYER=Talk to God.

SUPPLICATION=Be humbly specific when talking to God.

THANKSGIVING= The giving of thanks before you ever see anything happen.

Remember, you are living and walking by faith and not by sight or reveled by the senses.

- What are you to let/allow to happen? (Philippians 4:6)

NOTE: Remember that God already knowns what you need before you ask (Matthew 6:8) but He wants to ask Him.

- What is the cause and effect of your praying, supplicating and thanking God by faith in the face of anxiety? (Philippians 4:7)
- What kind of peace will you be given? (Philippians 4:7)
- What will be guarded? (Philippians 4:7)

1.

2.

- What will this guarding be in? (Philippians 4:7
- During times of anxiety, what should we allow/let our minds dwell on? (Philippians 4:8)

1.

2.

3.

4.

5.

6.

7.

8.

9.

Anxiety is logic on steroids and will destroy what your desires, dreams, visions, imaginations, inspirations, thoughts, ideas, goals, and plans. To be truly successful, learn the secret of busting anxiety instead of anxiety busting you.

TAKE THE TRAIN TO IMAGINATION STATION

*Casting down **imaginations**, and every high thing that exalts itself against the knowledge of God and bringing into captivity every thought to the obedience of Christ.*
                    ~2 Corinthians 10:5, emphasis mine

Y our *imagination* will imagine good or bad. Your imagination will imagine the worse case scenarios or imagine the best. If you don't take control of your imagination, it will take control of you.

IMAGINATION: logismos (*log-is-mos'*)=From G3049; *computation*, that is, (figuratively) *reasoning* (*conscience, conceit*): - imagination, thought. G3049: logizomai (*log-id'-zom-ahee*)=Middle voice from G3056; to *take an inventory*, that is, *estimate* (literally or figuratively): - conclude, (ac-) count (of), + despise, esteem, impute, lay, number, reason, reckon, suppose, think (on). **G3056: logos *(log'-os)*=**From G3004; something *said* (including the *thought*); by implication a *topic* (subject of discourse), also *reasoning* (the mental faculty) or *motive*; by extension a *computation*; specifically (with the article in John) the Divine *Expression* (that is, *Christ*): - account, cause, communication, X concerning, doctrine, fame, X have to do, intent, matter, mouth, preaching, question, reason, + reckon, remove, say (-ing), shew, X speaker, speech, talk, thing, + none of these things move me, tidings, treatise, utterance, word, work. **G3004: legō (*leg'-o)*=**A primary verb; properly to "lay" forth, that is, (figuratively) *relate* (in words [usually of systematic or set *discourse*; whereas G2036 and G5346 generally refer to an *individual* expression or speech respectively;

while G4483 is properly to *break silence* merely, and G2980 means an *extended* or random harangue]); by implication to *mean:* - ask, bid, boast, call, describe, give out, name, put forth, say (-ing, on), shew, speak, tell, utter.

Imagination starts off with a *thought* where you take an inventory about what you are thinking and then progresses from thought to words. When your imagination is expressed and then actions are based on your *imagination* this is where manifestation takes place. The results can be good, bad, or ugly based on what you are imagining.

We have the responsibility to take control our thoughts and what we speak and what we do.

In the Bible, Genesis 11:1–9 we see an example of people who spoke the same language/word and utilized their *imaginations*, to their detriment.

> *And the lord came down to see the city and the tower which the sons of men had built (starting with their imaginations and same language. And the Lord said, behold they are one people, and they have all one language; and this is only the beginning of what they will do, and how nothing they have* **IMAGINED** *they can do will be impossible for them.*
> ~Genesis 11:5–6 Amplified Bible emphasis mine

They had a **"CAN DO"** attitude, but the problem is that what they **"COULD DO"** was not what God wanted *DONE.* Their *imaginations* were based on fear of what might happen.

> *And they said (using one language), come, let us build us a city and a tower whose top reaches into the sky, and let us make a name for ourselves, lest we* **BE SCATTERD** *over the earth.*
> ~Genesis 11:3 emphasis mine

They were like Job in the sense that what he *thought about,* what he *imagined, came upon him.*

For what I fear comes upon me and what I dread befalls me . I am not at rest, but turmoil comes upon me.

~Job 3:25–26

Come let Us go down and there **CONFUSE** *their language, that they may not understand one another's speech (about what they imagined) so the Lord* **SCATTRED** *them (what they had feared) abroad from there over the face of the earth; and they stopped building the city. Therefore, its name was called Babel (bay-bull), because there the Lord confused the language of the whole earth; and from there the Lord* **SCATTERED** *them (what they feared) abroad over the face of the whole earth.*

~Genesis 11:7–9 addition and emphasis mine

I am convinced that if the people of Shinar had *captured their negative imaginations*, their outcome would be different.

The same is true for us in this day and age of *success and failure*. One of the *secrets of success* is to be able to strategically use our imaginations.

Casting down **imaginations**, *and every high thing that exalts itself against the knowledge of God and bringing into captivity every thought to the obedience of Christ.*

~2 Corinthians 10:5 emphasis mine

1. Casting down *imaginations*: Don't just let your *imaginations* run wild and out of control. Take authority over your *imagination*. Cast it down, put it in its place.
2. And every high thing that exalts itself against the knowledge of God: High things are aka lofty things and are aka prideful things. We are called to humble ourselves, humble our high things, humble our lofty things, humble our pride. (1 Peter 5:6–7)
3. And bringing into captivity *every thought* (what you think that is contrary to God thoughts).
4. To the obedience of God: Disobedience was in the Garden,

obedience was on the Cross by Jesus. When we take imaginations, high things, exalted things, prideful things and submit them to God, then our imaginations can be useful for our success.

HAVE A PURPOSE

*The Son of God came for this **purpose**, to destroy the works of the d-evil.*

~1 John 3:8, emphasis mine

PURPOSE: touto (*too'-to)*= thing: - here [-unto], it, partly, self [-same], so, that (intent), the same, there [-fore, -unto], this, thus, where [-fore].

IF you don't have *a purpose* then you will accomplish what you have or don't have, nothing (no thing, nada, zip, zilch, zero).

When our *purpose* lines up with God/Jesus' *purpose*, then we will have true prosperity and success. Remember that Biblical prosperity and success is defined as:

PROSPERITY: Having enough to meet your needs (not greed) and an overflow to help others.

SUCCESS: Accomplishing the purposes of God in your life.

When your *purpose* lines up Jesus' *purpose*, to destroy the works of the d-evil, then your *purpose* (whatever it is) has a whole new meaning.

If you desire, dream, imagination is to be the best salesman in whatever field you have chosen, then your purpose is to be a salesman who destroys the works of the d-evil. How will that be manifested in your life? I believe that as you increase in your sales, more money will come into your life and your bills will be paid, your house payment will be made, your refrigerator will be full, the nature of the flesh (the carnal nature) in your life will be broken and you will begin to live a life and walk a life of faith as the *spirit of poverty* will be broken in your life and you will have an overflow to help others meet their needs. That is only the beginning as you walk in te secret to success. When your purpose lines up with God' purpose in your life, you will begin to accomplish the purposes of God in your life versus allowing the purposes of the d-evil to dominate your life.

> *Beloved, I pray that you may prosper in every way and [that your body] may keep well, even as [I know] your soul keeps will and prospers.*
> ~3 John 2 Amplified Bible

I believe that the *purpose* of God, this destroying the works of the d-evil in your life deals with prosperity, health, and emotional prosperity. I believe that this prosperity and success will touch every area of your being, your (1) spirit=communication with God (2) soul=you mind (what you think) your volition (what you freely choose) and your body=your physical being, your health.

> *Now may the God of peace (wholeness, rest, no anxiety) Himself (involved in your life) entirely (not just a part); and may your spirit/ soma=communication with God, and your soul/psuche= your mind (what you think), your volition (what you freely choose base on what you think) and your body/soma= (your physical body that houses your spirit and our soul) be preserved complete, without blame at the coming of the Lord.*
> ~1 Thessalonians 5:23 with emphasis, additions and commentary mind, Ruminator Style

When you have a *purpose* (good, bad, or ugly), when you do these things "*on purpose*" then those things will come to you. The Law (principle) of Attraction (magnetizing) which is a universal law based on frequency and vibration is enacting, then good, bad, or ugly is attracted to you as you open the door by your free will of what you think, speak and do.

Whatsoever (good, bad or ugly) a man sows (plants in the ground and/or the universe) that shall he also reap (harvest).

"IF you sow seeds of poison ivy, then poison ivy is what you will reap. If you sow poison ivy and reap a crop of poison ivy, don't wonder why you have developed a rash."

~Rodfucious

As long as you think failure you will fail.

As a man thinketh in his heart/mind SO he is.
~Pro-Verbs 23:7 emphasis, additions, commentary mine,Ruminator Style

As a man thinketh failure/success in his heart **SO** *he is a failure or success.*
~Pro-Verbs 23:7 with emphasis, additions, commentary mine, Ruminator Style

Out of the abundance (overflow) of the heart/mind the mouth speaks (failure or success).
~Luke 6:45 emphasis, additions, commentary mine, Ruminator Style

Faith without corresponding actions (what you do) is of none effect (dead).
~James 2:17 Weymouth Translation with emphasis, additions, commentary mine, Ruminator Style

When you line up with God's purpose in any area of your life, and you begin to think God thoughts, speak God words, and do God things, the you will begin to fulfill God's purpose in your life, to destroy the works of the d-evil.

The thief comes to steal, kill and destroy but I (Jesus) came to give you life and that more abundantly.
~John 10:10 addition mine

The d-evil comes to steal your dreams, kill your visions, and destroy your imaginations **BUT** I (Jesus) came to give you an abundant life and destroy the works of the d-evil in your life.

~John 10:10 with emphasis, addition, and commentary mine, Ruminator Style)

I often ask people some questions:
1. What do you really want?
2. What are you willing to do to get what you really want?
3. What are the obstacles/obstructions keeping you from what you really want?
4. Are you just satisfied (settling) with your mediocre life or are you content with your God life?
5. What are the obstacles, obstructions, mountains (made by you, d-evil attacks) that are keeping from getting what you really want?
6. What are your excuses for not getting what you really want?
7. What are your legitimate reasons for not getting what you really want?
8. Who do you blame for not getting what you really want?

Your answers and your actions will determine if you get failure or success. What do you really want and what are you will to do to get success?

EXHIBIT THE ATTITUDE OF A SERVANT

Have this attitude in yourselves which was also in Christ Jesus, who, although He existed in the form of God, did not regard equality with God a thing to be grasped, but emptied Himself, taking the form of a bond-servant and being made in the likeness of men. Being found in appearance as a man, He humbled Himself by becoming obedient to the point of death, even death on a cross.
~Philippians 2:5–8

ATTITUDE/MIND: phroneō (*fron-eh'-o)*=From G5424; to *exercise* the *mind*, that is, *entertain* or *have* a *sentiment* or *opinion*; by implication to *be* (mentally) *disposed* (more or less earnestly in a certain direction); intensively to *interest oneself* in (with concern or obedience): - set the affection on, (be) care (-ful), (be like-, + be of one, + be of the same, + let this) mind (-ed, regard, savour, think. G5424: phrēn (*frane)*=Probably from an obsolete φράω phraō (to *rein* in or *curb*; compare G5420); the *midrif* (as a *partition* of the body), that is, (figuratively and by implication of sympathy) the *feelings* (or sensitive nature; by extension [also in the plural] the *mind* or cognitive faculties): - understanding.

ATTITUDE: (1) a settled way of thinking or feeling about someone or something, typically one that is reflected in a person's behavior= a point of view, viewpoint, vantage point, frame of mind (2) a position of the body proper to or implying an action or mental state=position, posture, pose, stance, stand, bearing (3) truculent or uncooperative behavior; a resentful or antagonistic manner (4) individuality and self-confidence as manifested by behavior or appearance; style: (5)

the orientation of an aircraft or spacecraft, relative to the direction of travel. (6) In ballet: a position in which one leg is lifted behind with the knee bent at right angles and turned out, and the corresponding arm is raised above the head, the other extended to the side. (Various dictionary definitions)

Your attitude follows your *paradigm/mindset*, and you will need to have a **paradigm shift and mindset change** before you can have success. The Secret is that you have to choose to have an *attitudinal adjustment.*

Jesus had an attitude, and it was the secret to His success. Jesus' secret was the attitude of being a servant.

- Jesus existed in the form of God. Jesus was in the beginning, was with God and WAS God. (John 1:1)

NOTE: Jesus could have stayed in heaven and not come down to die for our sins, but His heartbeat was one of obedience to the Father.

- Jesus did not regard equality with God a thing to be grasped. (Philippians 2:5)

NOTE: I tend to grasp, hold onto my spirituality. I tend to think that my level of spirituality places me above others where they need to serve me and not me serve them.

- **BUT** emptied Himself (Philippians 2:6–7)

NOTE: Most of us are full of ourselves leaving no room for others. When we are full of ourselves, we want others to serve us.

- Taking the form of a bond-servant and being made in the likeness of men. (Philippians 2:7)

SERVANT/BOND-SERVANT doulos (*doo'-los)*=From G1210; a *slave* (literally or figuratively, involuntarily or voluntarily; frequently therefore in a qualified sense of *subjection* or *subserviency*): - bond

(-man), servant. **G1210: deō (*deh'-o*)**=A primary verb; to *bind* (in various applications, literally or figuratively): - bind, be in bonds, knit, tie, wind.

NOTE: When we serve others, we are serving God. A servant is someone who is bound with the commitment to serve the master. A bond-servant is said to be a servant who has been set free but chooses to continue to serve even though they don't have to.

- And being made in the likeness of men (Philippians 2:7)

NOTE: This is what Jesus did, He was God (John 1:1) but in obedience became God in the flesh and dwelt among us (John 1:14)

- Being found in appearance as a man, He humbled Himself by becoming obedient to the point of death, even death on a cross. (Philippians 2:8)

NOTE: Jesus' point of humility, his point of obedience was when He allowed Himself to be nailed on a cross in our place become a curse in our place. We identify with this point of death (Galatians 2:20) daily, as we choice to die to ourselves every single day. (1 Corinthians 15:31) It is only then that we can become servants of success in our obedience to Him.

> *He who has my commandments and keeps them He it is who loves Me, and he who loves Me, and He who loves me will be loved by my Father and I will love him and will manifest, reveal, disclose Myself to him.*
>
> ~John 14:21 with emphasis, additions and commentary mine

IF you can figure out to serve others, you will have learned the secret to success. Read the book by Gayle Erwin, *The Jesus Style* for more information on how to be successful in your spiritual life and your life in general.

LEAVE THE OLD AND LIVE IN THE NEW

The steadfast love of the Lord never ceases, His mercies never comes to an end, they are new every morning, great is Thy faithfulness.
~Lamentations 3:22–23

God's love never ceases.

God's mercies never comes to an end.

They (God's love and mercies) are **NEW** every morning.

His faithfulness is **GREAT**.

I love this lament by Jeremiah. Every single, every single day that I get up is another opportunity to start over, to correct the mistakes, to learn the lessons, to continue forward to success.

This is the day that the Lord has made, let us rejoice and be glad in it."
~Psalm 118:24

This is the day (Tuesday, June 6th, 2023, at the time of this writing) that the Lord has made, let us (me and you) rejoice (spin around under a violent emotion, choose to be glad and joyful) and be glad (not sad, brighten up, make merry, be joyful, full of joy) in it (Tuesday, June 6th, 2023, at the time of this writing).
~Psalm 118:24, with emphasis, additions, commentary mine, Ruminator Style

There is a 24-hour cycle where we can start over, forget the mistakes, learn the lessons, and go back at it. We live one breath at time, we walk one step at a time, we exist one day at a time (sweet Jesus), and we accomplish our desires, dreams, visions, imaginations, inspirations, thoughts, ideas, goals, and plans one moment at a time. We get to start over every 24 hours which leads us to failure or success.

I like the philosophy that Jeff Suter (of CMG Mortgage Company) lives by; "live the refined life." Every day, he gets up and does the things that needs to be done for that day to accomplish his purposes, to be successful. This thing called the "Refined Life" is nothing but the "Abundant Life," the Successful Life," the life with the impurities or unwanted elements have been removed processing, many times by fire. Note that the process is not instant gratification, but a daily process where we have to die to ourselves and live to Him.

> *Therefore if any man is in Christ, he is a new creation, the old things passed away; behold, new (and fresh) things have come (are constantly coming)."*
>
> ~2 Corinthians 5:17 addition mine

I like that this applies to any man/woman/human.
I like that we can live daily in the new and not the old.
I like that new and fresh things are constantly coming.

> *He made Him who knew no sin to be sin on our behalf, that we might become the righteousness of God in Him.*
>
> ~2 Corinthians 5:21

We are all sinners and unrighteous (Roman 3:23)
Jesus knew no sin but became sin in our place on the cross.
We became righteous because of Him.
Our righteousness is the righteousness of God in Jesus.

> *That which is born of the flesh is flesh, and that which is born of the Spirit is spirit. Do not marvel that I said to you, you must be born again.*
>
> ~John 3:6–7

If He said I must be, then I must be.
No need for marveling about what He said.
I can either live and die in the flesh or LIVE in the Spirit.

Therefore we have been buried with Him through baptism into death, in order that as Christ was raised from the dead through the glory of the Father; so we too might walk in newness of life.
~Romans 6:4

Baptism is the picture/likeness of the real deal, the D.B.R., D=Death B=Burial R=Resurrection. Jesus raised from the dead so that I can walk in newness of life.

I am convinced that the principles that we have been talking about works for the Christian, the non-Christian, the atheist, the agnostic, the pagan, the religious person, the spiritual person (all the whosoevers that God so loved), however, to experience the full impact of prosperity and success, the # 1 Secret is the #32 Secret, an intimate relationship with the Creator of the universe.

THE SECRET OF PROSPERITY AND SUCCESS PARADIGM/MINDSET

A **PARADIGM/MINDSET** is a mental pattern that affects your habitual behaviors (good, bad, ugly) in the way that you think, speak and act (good, bad, ugly) and brings the R.A.M.=Results, Achievements and Manifestations in your life.

> *As a man thinketh in his heart/mind* ***SO HE IS***.
> ~Pro-Verbs 23:7 addition and emphasis mine

NOTE: The thoughts that you dwell on, that you focus on, that you think about will translate into who you are, the type of person that you are.

> *Out of the abundance (overflow) of the heart/mind the* ***MOUTH SPEAKS***.
> ~Luke 6:45 addition and emphasis mine

NOTE: Your heart/mind is filled with whatever you are thinking about and overflows out of your mouth. You mouth is the great revealer of what you really believe, especially when you are shaken by external events.

> ***FAITH*** *(what you believe=trust in, cling to, rely on, adhere to, cleave to)* ***WITHOUT*** *(null and void of)* ***CORRESPONDING*** *(lining up with your faith/belief)* ***ACTIONS*** *(deeds/works) is of* ***NONE*** *(zip, zero, zilch, nada, no, no thing, nothing)* ***EFFECT***

(effectual outcomes.)

~James 2:17 additions and emphasis mine

NOTE: When you hear the Word, faith comes. (Romans 10:17) IF you just hear the Word and then don't do the Word then your faith is null and void and ineffective.

*The **MIND SET** (a verb of focus that will turn into your **MIND-SET**) on the **FLESH** (carnal nature, negativity, d-evil thoughts) is **DEATH** (separation from God) **BUT** (in contrast to) the **MIND SET** (a verb of focus that will turn into your **MINDSET**) on the Spirit (the Holy Spirit, positivity, God thoughts, His Word) is **LIFE** (and that more abundantly/overflowing) and **PEACE** (wholeness, rest, no anxiety, not fear, not worry, no doubt).*

~Romans 8:6 additions and emphasis mine

NOTE: Your **MINDSET/PARADIGM** does not just magically appear. It is the product of spiritual, physical, emotional **D.N.A./ Genetics** passed down from the Garden of Eden to you. (Romans 5:12) Once you are born, your **MINDSET/PARADIGM** continues to be develop by your surrounding environment (good, bad, ugly) via your lower faculties including your sight, sound, smell, taste, and touch. You have a choice to focus on the negative or focus on the positive. You choice will determine the **R.A.M.=Results, Achievements, Manifestations in** your life. Focus on the flesh=death. Focus on the Spirit= life and peace. Which one do you want in your life. I believe that if you focus on various topics, you will develop a certain **PARADIGM/MINDSET** (Good, Bad, Ugly). For example, if you constantly focus on poverty, you will open the door to poverty by what you think, speak, and do. You will have developed a **POVERTY PARADIGM/MINDSET.** If you constantly think, speak and act like a failure, you will develop a **FAILURE PARADIGM/MINDSET.** Plug in anything into your mind, start speaking that way and start acting that way habitually, start seeing changes in your R.A.M.= Results, Achievements, Manifestations.

These principles of the **PROSPERITY** and **SUCCESS PARADIGM/MINDSET** are not some tool of manipulation to get from God, however the principle/law of **RECIPROCITY** of giving and getting is outlined from Jesus, "**GIVE** and *it shall be* **GIVEN UNTO YOU**…" (Luke 6:38) Traditions of men have taught us that *"you don't give to get."* Well, yes you do. No, you don't **LUST** after money to get more money to lavish on yourself, that is the "**ROOT OF ALL KINDS OF EVIL,** and by it (the lust/love of money) some by longing for it have wandered away from the faith and pierced themselves with many a pang. (1 Timothy 6:10) The next verse speaks of how to deal with these things. "But flee from these things, you man of God; and pursue righteousness, godliness, faith, love, perseverance and gentleness." (1 Timothy 6:11)

Many Christians believe that the more poor that they are correlates with their spirituality. Some go to the extreme of taking a *"vow of poverty."* I believe that *poverty is a curse,* and I refuse to take a *"vow of a curse."* I personally take a "vow of a blessing."

Imagine filtering prosperity and success, money, wealth, things through righteousness, godliness, faith, love, perseverance, and gentleness, and you become a steward of those things instead of holding tightly to them. Instead of being **GO-GETTERS** you become a **GO-GIVER.** Poverty is a curse and Prosperity is a blessing. Have people abused these principles, yes, but that does not negate the principles of prosperity and success, especially when you mediate on the Word of God 7/24/365 and then **DO THE WORD.** You can have, you must have an **EXPECTANCY** of God meeting your **NEEDS** (not your greed) according to His riches in **GLORY** and in **CHRIST JESUS** (and there ain't no shortage in His glory and in The Anointed One and His anointing. (Philippians 4:19)

NO, we don't deny reality of the world, but we do deny reality's right to rule our life, our present, our future and yes our destiny. NO, I don't believe that every Christian will have loads of money, a new car, a Roth I.R.A., fill in the blank with every material thing that you can imagine. I know many people who have "learned to be content in whatever circumstance" that they are in and they "know how to get along with humble means , and I/they know how-to **LIVE-IN**

PROSPERITY in **ANY** and **EVERY CIRCUMSTANCE.**" (Philippians 4:11–12) They have "learned **THE SECRET** of being filled and going hungry, both of having **ABUNDANCE** and **SUFFERING.**" (Philippians 4:12) This thought process leads us to Philippians 4:13 and Philippians 4:19.

*I have **STRENGTH** for all things in Christ Who **EMPOWERS** me [I am ready for anything and equal to anything through Him Who infuses **INNER STRENGTH** into me; I am self-sufficient **IN CHRIST'S SUFFICIENCY.**"*
Philippians 4:13 Amplified Bible emphasis mine

*And my God will **LIBERALLY SUPPLY** (fill to the full) your every **NEED** according to His riches in glory in Christ Jesus.*
~Philippians 4:19 Amplified Bible emphasis mine

NOTE: This **STRENGTH** and **SUPPLY** is about money/wealth/needs/circumstances, prosperity, suffering, humble means, being filled, going hungry, contentment, attitude I believe that it is not the **CIRCUMSTANCE** but **the PARADIGM/MINDSET/ATTITUDE**, trusting God.

I have five verses that I choose to focus on, set my mind on, ruminate about concerning finances, money, things, stuff, needs, wealth, Pro-Vision (Positive Revelatory Insights) to prosperity and success.

This essay is a thumbnail sketch about these principles. I go into details in my books in **THE SUCCESS SERIES:**
How To Live A Maximized Life
Biblical Prosperity and Success
Thirty-Two Secrets To The Not So Secret, Secrets of Success

THE WORD, PROSPERITY, AND SUCCESS

This book of the Law (the Word) shall not depart from your mouth, but you shall meditate on it day and night, so that you may be

careful to do all that is written in it, for then you will make your
way prosperous and then you will have (good) success."

Joshua 1:8) additions mine

NOTE: The key to Biblical Prosperity and Success is The Word of God. You must speak the Word of God (mutter under your breath) day and night. That does not mean that you are constantly talking 7/24/365, but it does mean that you are always ready to speak it in whatever situation/circumstance (good, bad, ugly) that arises. Unless you choose to meditate/ruminate on the Word of God, you will not have anything to speak other than your own thoughts or the thoughts of the world system or d-evil thoughts. Then you must be careful in the sense of not just being cavalier about the Word of God. You must be careful to **DO** (put into action the Word of God in your life. The cause and effect of meditating on the Word of God and doing the Word of God will be **PROSPERITY** and **SUCCESS**.

BIBLICAL PROSPERITY: Having enough to meet your needs (not your greed) and an overflow to help others. (Luke 6:38, 1 Corinthians 9:11–18)

BIBLICAL SUCCESS: Accomplishing the purpose of God in your life which includes lining up with the purpose of Jesus, to "destroy the works of the d-evil." (I John 3:8)

STRENGTH AND SUPPLY

*"I can do **ALL THINGS** through Christ Who strengthens me.*
~Philippians 4:13

NOTE: The people who say I **CAN** do, and I **CAN'T** DO are both correct. I believe that **ALL THINGS** means **ALL THINGS**. It is through Christ (the Anointed One and His anointing of the Holy Spirit and Power (dunamis, dynamic miracle ability) where our strength comes from in our weakness. (Romans 8:26, 2 Corinthians 12:9–10, Joel 3:10)

Before the children of Israel were going to cross over into the Promised Land filled with giants, there are nine time (in Deuteronomy and Joshua) where the phrase, "be strong and courageous is found. (Deuteronomy 31:6–7, Deuteronomy 31:23, Joshua 1:6–7, Joshua 1:9, Joshua 1:18, Joshua 10:25) **WHY?** Because they would have every opportunity to be weak and discouraged. Then the phrase "do not tremble or be dismayed" occurs in Joshua 1:9. **WHY?** Because they were going to have every opportunity to tremble/shake and be dismayed/not believe what they are seeing (giants).

There must be *preparation* and *expectation*.

> *Prepare provisions for yourselves, for within three days you are to cross this Jordan to go in to possess the land which the Lord your God is giving you, to possess it (where you will have opportunities to be weak and discourage and tremble and be dismayed).*
> ~Joshua 1:11 additions mine

> *Then Joshua said to the people (who were about to cross the Jordan) consecrate (set yourself aside for the purposes of God) yourselves (today, implied) for tomorrow the Lord will do wonders among you.*
> ~Joshua 1:5 additions mine

There preparation was **THE WORD OF GOD.** I believe as we develop various **PARADIGMS** and **MINDSETS** we are renewing our minds with the Word of God concerning whatever we need. We begin to *think/mediate*; we begin to *speak/confess,* and we begin to *do/corresponding actions* to what we *believe/have faith* about.

SUPPLY CHAIN ECONOMICS

> *And my God shall supply all your needs according to His riches in glory and in Christ Jesus.*
> ~Philippians 4:19

NOTE: God is in charge of our supply. God's economy is not "trickle down economics." A song by The Imperials declares when it comes to God's love, there is no shortage, even in the face of all the shortages in the world economy system. God supplies **ALL** our needs (not our greed). God's economy is not based on the world supply. The world tells us that there is a limited amount of supply and once that is gone there is no more supply.

The Maharishi (ma ha, ah ha think the Three Stooges) Yogi, the guru of the Beatles and many others, wanted to introduce to the world Transcendental (mystical, divine, non-natural) Meditation (a counterfeit to Biblical Meditation. (Joshua 1:8) His financial advisor (yes, this humble man had a financial advisor) told him that this would be very expensive and asked him, "Where will the money come from? The Maharishi said, "The money will come from wherever the money is." As wrong as the Maharishi was, he was right about this. There is unlimited supply in God's riches, in glory, in Christ Jesus.

NOTE: We are not only the "hearers" of the Word, but we must be the "doers" of the Word of God. (James 1:22–25) I want to hear what God says about prosperity and success. I want to hear what God says about supply and Pro-Vision (positive revelatory insights) into God's prosperity and success.

NOTE: Philippians 4:13 is the capstone of Paul's teaching about money/needs that I believe that applies to anything concerning God in my life. (Philippians 4:10–12, 14–18)

GOD'S RECIPROCITY

> *Give and it shall be given to you, good measure, pressed down, shaken together, running over shall men give into your bosom/lap.*
> ~Luke 6:38 addition mine

NOTE: Many people say that we **DO NOT** give to get. Well, I understand but, that is not what Jesus is teaching. Reciprocity means: (1) The practice of exchanging things with others for mutual benefit, especially privileges granted by one country or organization to another. (2) an in and out action like a reciprocating saw. (3) the act of sowing and reaping.

Jesus teaches that if you do this then that will happen. Give (whatever) and it shall be (not might be, not maybe, but shall be) it (whatever you gave) shall **BE GIVEN** to you. Luke 6:38 about being a giver and in return getting more than you gave back, is the capstone on Jesus' teaching about reciprocity. (Luke 6:27–27)

Some was trying to put down Bob Proctor (motivational teacher) by saying, "Oh you are one of those Go-Getters!" Bob immediately responded, No, I am a Go-Giver. Bob knew the secret of giving and you will get. I am convince that when you let go of your money and walk by faith and not by sight (Galatians 5:7) that money will return to you by the hand of man. God uses men to provide His provision. "shall men give into your bosom/lap/basket." (Luke 6:38)

SEED FOR THE SOWER

Now this I say, he who sows sparingly shall also reap sparingly
and he who sows bountifully shall also reap bountifully.
> ~2 Corinthians 9:6

NOTE: 2 Corinthians 9:5–15 is a blueprint of how to give money away with the expectancy of receiving money back. I am not talking about tithing (giving of 10% which is an Old Testament Principle that is a good starting point, but about giving beyond the tithe. I personally believe that we are released from the tithe into giving, which if you are a true giver, will probably be more than your tithe. Here is a breakdown of 2 Corinthians 9:5–15 about being a sower.

1. Arrange before hand a promise, bountiful gift to avoid covetousness (where if you think about it you may not give. (2 Corinthians 9:5)
2. The amount that you sow (money) affects the amount that you receive. Sow (give) sparingly, reap (get) sparingly. Sow

(give) bountifully, reap (get) bountifully. (2 Corinthians 9:6)

3. Purpose in your heart the amount that you give. Don't be like Ananias and Saphira who sold their land and pretended to give all to the poor but held a portion back. (Acts 5:1–10) Peter confronted them about their deception and said, "While it (the land) remained unsold, did it not remain your own? And after it was sold, was it not under your control? You have not lied to men, but to God." A & S were **NOT** *cheerful givers*. The cause and effect for them was death. (Acts 5:5–10) When you give don't give (1) grudgingly (2) under compulsion. God loves a cheerful (hilarious) giver. I believe that as you horde money, you may have stuff, but you will be sick physically. (2 Corinthians 9:7)

4. Realize That God is able! When we are not able, God is able. He has the ability to do what it takes. God is able to make grace (unmerited favor, a free gift, the divine influence inside you to be manifested outwardly) *ABOUND* to you. When you give you can have (1) All sufficiency in everything (2) An abundance for every good deed. (2 Corinthians 5:8) his promise is based on Psalm 112:9. (2 Corinthians 9:8-9) "He scattered abroad, He gave to the poor, His righteousness abides forever." (Psalm 112:9)

5. Know that God is the Seed Supplier supplying seed to the sower. The seed is money. He also supplies bread for food. He will *SUPPLY* and *MULTIPLY* your seed for sowing (giving). He will *INCREASE* the harvest of your righteousness (right standing with God based on the standard who God is). A standard in the circus world is the center post by which all guidelines are attached to that hold the tent up. (2 Corinthians 9:10)

6. Understand that you will be enriched (augmented, supplemented, improved) in everything (in every area of your life including money) for all liberality (broadmindedness, kindness, generosity). When do these things, it produces in us thanksgiving (the giving of thanks to God). (2 Corinthians 9:11)

7. Many people are looking for a "ministry," a calling, a purpose,

and a destiny. Our ministry is supplying the needs of the saints. Remember, Biblical Prosperity is having enough to met your needs (that God gives you as you give) and an overflow to others. Abundance means an overflow). (2 Corinthians 9:12)

8. People see your giving and glorify God. They see not only what you are saying, but what you do when you put your faith into actions. Confession means say the same word that God says, coming into agreement with God. Our confession is about the Death, Burial, and Resurrection of Jesus, the Gospel, 1 Corinthians 15:1–5) Our relationship to Jesus is the basis of their liberality of their contributions to others. (2 Corinthians 9:13)

9. When you give, people are praying or you and yearn for you because of the surpassing grace of God in you. The word *BLESSED* means to be supremely happy so as to be envied by others as they *SEE* your life-joy, satisfaction, salvation *REGARDLESS* of your *CURRENT CIRCUMSTANCES*. As they see your generosity, the want what you've got. (2 Corinthians 9:14)

10. Thanks be to God for His indescribable gift of Jesus that He gave us because He so loved the World. Believe (trust in, cling to, rely on, adhere to, cleave to) Jesus. (John 3:16, 2 Corinthians 9:15)

*And let each one who is **taught the Word share all good things with him who teaches.** Do not be deceived, God is not mocked; for **WHATEVER** a man **SOWS**, this he will also **REAP**. For the one who **SOWS** to the flesh shall from the flesh reap corruption, but the one who **SOWS** to the Spirit shall from the Spirit **REAP** eternal life. And let us not **LOSE HEART** in doing good, for in due time we shall **REAP IF WE DO NOT GROW WEARY**."*
~Galatians 6:6–9 emphasis mine

NOTE: Reciprocity, seedtime, and harvest, sowing and reaping, giving, and receiving, casting your bread on the water with the expectation that what you cast (gave) will come back to you.

*While the earth remains, seedtime and harvest, and cold and heat, and simmer and winter, and day and night shall **NOT CEASE**.*
~Genesis 8:22 emphasis mine

These principles were "in the beginning" and they still work in 2023 (when this was written).

- You are being *taught* the Word. As a teacher, I love that part of sowing and reaping is giving to the teacher. I lead through **RODNEY LEWIS BOYD SERVICES** (How May I Serve You and the World God So Loves?) and part of that is through teaching. My financial policy is (a) A laborer is worthy of his hire (Luke 10:27, 1 Timothy 5:18, Matthew 10:10) (b) You pray and you obey. Part of your giving is to share all good things with him who teaches. (Galatians 6:6)

NOTE: Even as I write this, I hesitate because people might think that I am writing this to manipulate people to give money to me, but that is not why I am writing it, however, God told me once that I don't have to beg for places to speak or beg for money. Then He spoke to me to prepare a place to receive money when people have prayed, and they want to obey.

- Deception and mocking is when you don't sow into others and don't expect God to give back to you. Whatever (it does not matter what) you sow (give) you can expect that you will reap (get back). (Galatians 6:7)
- Be careful where you sow your seed. If you sow your seed to the flesh (your carnal nature) then you will be reaping the exact fruit of the seed that you sowed. You don't want to reap corruption. If you sow into the soil of the Spirit get ready to reap from the Spirit eternal life. Sure, eternal life is heaven, but I am convinced that as soon as you step into the streams of salvation, you have stepped into the streams of salvation to live your life. (Galatians 6:9)
- I know that when you begin to sow (whatever from money to love) when you don't see immediate results you get discouraged

and want to give up. We are told to **NOT LOSE HEART**. (1 Corinthians 15:58, 1 Corinthians 4:1) There is a song by a Jesus Music group from the 70s that had a song called **KEEP ON WALKING**. It asks the question about being weary in well doing as we live out our life here on earth pre-heaven and encourages us to keep walking because we just don't know how far we've come, and any minute, the Lord will return. The same is true for sowing and reaping. We may sow our seed and not see immediate reaping. While the seed is underground, it is dying, sprouting roots, growth is taking place underground before it breaks through the soil. But even then there is no harvest, that comes with time. We don't give up; we don't dig up the seed to see what is going on. In the spiritual and in the natural we walk (live) by faith and not by sight. (2 Corinthians 5:7)

Give, Give, Give, Sow, Sow, Sow and Reap, Reap, Reap, and don't give up, keep expecting a harvest expect to get, be a *Go-Giver* and also be a *Go-Getter*.

Well, we have scratched the surface of *31 Secrets of the not so Secret, Secrets of Success.* If you just sit down and read the 31 Secrets, you can complete the book in 31 days.

However, if you are like me, you will start reading the book, and begin to underline phrases, circle words, write in the margin and most likely get sidetracked by the leading of God, and it may take more than 31 days. I know that as I was writing the book, I became distracted to thinking of many other secrets to success. I probably could have gone for 365 days of secrets to success, but for now 31 days will suffice.

I believe that this new book is wonderful (full of wonder). I must admit that although I wrote the book, as I was proofreading the manuscript, I was taken aback. This is a pretty darn good book, if I do say so myself! Out of my previous eleven books, this one could be my favorite (although that is a bit like choosing your favorite child).

While it might sound like shameless self-promotion, I do recommend the entire Success Trilogy, which includes: *How To Live a Maximized Life, Biblical Prosperity and Success: Ruminator Style*, and *Thirty-one Secrets to the not so Secret, Secrets of Success*—because I truly believe the principles presented in these books can help you live a better, more fulfilled, and yes, more successful life.

My prayer is that this book will encourage you to dig deep into the Word of God and realize that the world's success is superficial, but the success of God has deep roots that will establish Kingdom Roots where in your personal life, your professional life will be established on the rock of Christ (the Anointed One and His Anointing) and as the world's shifting sand of so called success is washed away; you will be living in true prosperity and success based on the Solid Rock.

ABOUT THE AUTHOR

Rodney Boyd is first and foremost a follower of Jesus Christ. He is also a husband, dad and speech-language pathologist. Rodney holds a Master's Degree in Education with emphasis in Speech Communication and has been a practicing Speech-Language Pathologist since 1993. He holds a 2nd degree Black Belt in Wado Ryu Karate; has a passion for music of all styles; and enjoys writing, teaching the Word of God.

Rodney has been married to his high school sweetheart, Brenda, for more than 51 years and together they have one son, Phillip, a daughter-in-law, Jamie, and one granddaughter, Emerson Grace (How Sweet The Sound) Boyd.

Boyd bases his life on Colossians 3:17, "And whatever you do in word or deed, do all in the name of the Lord Jesus, giving thanks through Him to God the Father."

Connect with Rodney on line at:

www.rodneylewisboyd.com

Aslo Available from
WordCrafts Press

Questing
by Wayne Berry

Positioned for Transition
by Barbie Loflin

Donkey Tales
by Keith Alexis

I AM
by Summer McKinney

What's the Big Idea?
by Robert G. Lee

www.wordcrafts.net